Tuning the Heart

University Sermons

Tuning the Heart

University Sermons

by C. Welton Gaddy

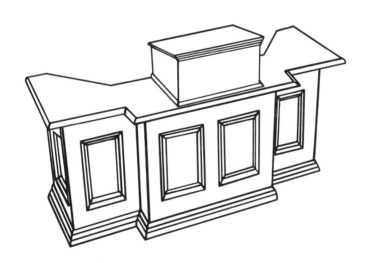

MERCER UNIVERSITY PRESS

ISBN 0-86554-367-4

The paper used in the publication meets
the minimum requirements of American National Standard
for Information Sciences—Permanence of Paper
for Printed Library Materials, ANSI Z39.48-1984.

Library of Congress Cataloging-in-Publication Data
Gaddy, C. Welton
Tuning the heart : university sermons / by C. Welton Gaddy.
xi + 179pp. 6 × 9″ (15 × 23cm)
ISBN 0-86554-367-4 (alk. paper)
1. Sermons, American.   2. Baptists—Sermons.
3. Southern Baptist Convention—Sermons.   I. Title.
BX6333.G23T85   1990   89-29749
252′.061—dc20   CIP

Contents

Christian Life

Christian Year

Foreword

It happened in a crossword puzzle in a Sunday edition of *The New York Times*. The definition for 21-across was "to moralize." A six-letter word was called for. The answer, it turned out, was "preach."

Well, moralizing is to preaching what astrology is to astronomy; what the Boy Scout motto is to John 3:16; what a cookbook is to a dinner invitation; what a Dale Carnegie course is to biblical religion.

But what can we expect? Preaching is an undervalued genre in our society. It is a performing art for which there is no Oscar. There is no Nobel prize for preaching. We have no preachers laureate on either side of the Atlantic. Or on either side of the Pacific, for that matter. The pejorative ring to the command, "Don't preach at me!" says it all.

Preaching may well be a loyalty under fire in our society, but it has never lost its importance for the church. Good things happen in congregations that celebrate preaching. Bad things happen where preaching is neglected. As a vital part of corporate worship, preaching bridges the gap between the "then and there" of Scripture and the "here and now" of contemporary life. It is the instrument most commonly used by the Holy Spirit to keep the story of God's love pulsing in our hearts. Karl Barth was not afraid to acclaim preaching as a form of transubstantiation: the written word, through the spoken word, becomes a living word. Fortunate indeed are those who live within weekly range of good preaching.

But good preaching doesn't just happen. It must be created. And there's the rub. The begetting of a sermon requires perspiration, inspiration, and courage. Perspiration, because to yield their treasure the Scriptures must be diligently exegeted. Inspiration, because without resolved dependence on the Holy Spirit one's words will have the shallow ring of chimes that tinkle with the wind. And courage, because there are gods out there to topple and idols that need to be upended. The human costs are high and few there are who are willing to pay the price.

All the more, then, do we welcome this collection of sermons from a preacher who has something to say and knows how to say it. These are not sermons addressed "To Whom It May Concern." We do not pick them up at the general delivery window of the post office. They are not generic in nature but helpfully specific. They come from the heart of a pastor who week by week spoke to a waiting university congregation.

Two of the five congregations that I served were located in an academic community. In my judgment, there is no more exciting a place in which to preach. The students keep one young. The faculty keeps one humble. References must be tight and accurate. The language must be clear. Conclusions must be honestly arrived at—no stolen bases.

But most of all, one gets caught up in the excitement of ministering to young people who have yet to answer those three important questions: What do I believe? What will I do with my life? Whom will I marry? In other words, one deals with human beings who are upstream, whose judgments and convictions are just now being formed.

Welton Gaddy's sermons reflect the stimulation of the university setting. In these messages one senses the outreach of a pastor who knows firsthand the faith he shares and who cares deeply for those with whom he shares it. I felt my own soul stirred and strengthened as I read these sermons. How thankful we should be that the few who heard originally will now have their ranks augmented by the many who will join them through the printed page. God be praised for preacher's art and printer's ink!

—Ernest T. Campbell

Preface

One crisp, rather cold afternoon in the early spring of 1984, Dr. Kirby Godsey, president of Mercer University, and I enjoyed a delightful visit with Dr. Louie Newton, a Baptist patriarch of international acclaim. While sitting together in Dr. Newton's home, Dr. Godsey explained the scope of the responsibilities related to the newly created position of Senior Minister to the University at Mercer. After all three of us had reaffirmed the religious heritage of this university and the importance of worship in its contemporary life, Dr. Newton raised his right hand, pointed directly at me, and said, "In that hymn, 'Come, Thou Fount of Every Blessing,' in the second phrase. . . . " Following a lengthy pause this sensitive old servant continued very deliberately, "tune my heart to sing Thy grace." Dr. Newton stopped, looked me squarely in the eyes and commented, "I'm glad you're here doing it."

On many occasions during my university-related ministry I recalled Dr. Newton's words for profitable reflection. Tuning the heart! I saw that joyous task requiring the serious discipline of structuring a context of authentic worship and within that setting grappling with the meaning of the gospel. Such a mission squared precisely with President's Godsey's articulated intention as he extended the invitation for me to do ministry within Mercer University.

"I want someone to read and study and interpret the gospel to a rather secular university." Those were Kirby Godsey's exact words of vision in our very first conversation about this new position within Mercer University. Early considerations of the responsibilities involved in this initiative produced a proposed title for the person to fill this position—"University Preacher." Frankly, I had problems with that. My strong conviction was and is that the best preaching grows out of a comprehensive ministry involving pastoral care, crisis intervention, community building, administrative decision making, and worship leadership. Dialogue concerning needs and hopes continued. Finally, discussion focused on a position entitled Senior Minister to the University. When Dr. Godsey extended to me an invitation to assume responsibility for that ministry, I happily accepted. Tuning the heart.

Almost every week for four and a half years I led worship and delivered sermons in chapel services on both the Macon and Atlanta campuses of Mercer University. In each instance I sought to make Newton Sanctuary in Macon or the Fine Arts Auditorium in Atlanta the nexus of biblical truths, personal problems, communal needs, pastoral concerns, and divine revelation. Printed copies of my messages were distributed to a larger congregation by means of a publication known as *The Mercer Pulpit.*

Numerous times I have been asked to name the differences which exist between preaching in a university setting and preaching in a local church. Quite honestly, I believe such differences are few in number. Spiritually speaking, the basic problems and most persistent needs of persons are the same in each place. Symptoms of difficulties, the vocabulary of personal expressions, and the specific dynamics of concern may differ between members of a local parish and citizens of academia. However, the truths in need of affirmation, elaboration, and application in each context do not vary.

The contents of this volume have been compiled in response to requests for this material to be presented and preserved in a more permanent medium. I make no special claims for what follows. I harbor no illusion regarding the uniqueness or exemplary nature of my work. I have stood on foundations constructed by scholars and preachers who are among my heroes in the faith. I have been helped by others who have ministered in a university context. I am indebted to far more thinkers than those whose names appear in the footnotes.

My willingness to allow the publication of these sermons stems from a genuine desire to join the pilgrimages of other believers and to contribute to the development of substantive convictions. These are "university sermons" only in the sense of the setting in which they were first delivered. The subject matter, support materials, and applications of these sermons are as broad as life. In every instance I have sought honestly to share the questions, affirmations, and struggles of my own faith with the hope of even minimally helping someone else similarly interested in redemption.

I must thank Dr. Kirby Godsey and members of the Board of Trustees of Mercer University for wisely placing a high priority on preaching and worship in the life of the institution, consistently hearing my words attentively, and faithfully responding to my ministry supportively. I am grateful as well for those persons—students, faculty members, and administrators—who attended university worship services voluntarily and expectantly. Encouragement from colleagues such as Walter Shurden, Rollin Armour, Wil Platt, Margaret Mueller, Timothy Wissler, and Betty Parsons within the university and persons like Bert Struby in the larger community has been invaluable. In this work as in all other endeavors I have been strengthened considerably by the gifts of my family—Judy, my wife, and our sons John Paul and James Welton.

One of the greatest joys of my life was the opportunity for a short time to associate with George Buttrick, another preacher who served within a university—perhaps one of the two greatest preachers in this century—to receive encouragement and instruction from him, and to call him my friend. With profound appreciation for Dr. Buttrick and identification with many of his convictions, I appropriate for myself some words which I had the good fortune to hear him speak: "The preacher . . . lives in no-man's-land, caught in a cruel cross fire: in one trench are those who can't stand change, in the other those who can't stand the Changeless. He is the dispensable man. His preaching when true is a sacrifice, an offering laid on an altar. He is content that it go up in flame and smoke. The sermon is therefore also a sacrament: 'the outward and visible sign of an inward and invisible grace,' in short God's gift to [people] through Christ. The preacher doesn't belong anywhere. Instead he belongs everywhere—to God in Christ. I'm proud and glad, though 'with fear and trembling,' that God has let me belong to the club."[1]

—*C. Welton Gaddy*

---

[1]George A. Buttrick, "Integrity In Preaching," *Integrity. 1975 Christian Life Commission Seminar Proceedings* (Nashville: The Christian Life Commission of the Southern Baptist Convention, 1975) 37.

Christian Faith

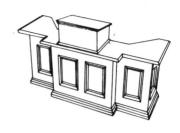

What Do You Believe?

What do you believe?

I plead with you to take that question seriously, to grapple with it honestly, and to stay with it tenaciously until you grasp some answer to it. What do you believe?

Please understand that I am not inquiring about what the Bible says, what your church affirms, or what doctrines you have been taught. My question is not what should you say or what would friends and family members want you to say. I am asking what you—you personally—believe—really believe. What do you believe?

Do not be alarmed if an answer does not come quickly—especially an honest answer. Most of us are programmed to respond to this kind of inquiry in a manner that sufficiently impresses those whom we want to impress. Thus, often responses are almost mechanical. We parrot certain memorized cliches even if they are devoid of personal meaning. Other individuals feel a necessity to answer such an inquiry in a manner agnostic enough to receive attention. They simply shrug their shoulders and state casually, "Nothing! I do not believe anything. I do not even fool around with that belief stuff." Well, so much for impressiveness. That is not my concern. I want no audible response from any of you, only a truthful, personal recognition of the situation within each of you. What do you believe? Answering the question may take some time.

Perhaps I should explain why I am so insistent upon your involvement with this question. The word "belief" comes from two old Anglo-Saxon words: "be" which meant "by" and "lief" which meant "life." Thus, belief is by-life. What one believes is what one lives by. Belief is the foundation upon which a person lives, the criterion by which a person decides

---

*This sermon was delivered to a congregation of freshmen gathered in a Sunday morning worship service during their orientation to the University before the beginning of classes.

how to live. In fact, as Carl Braaten has pointed out, find out what is cap-
italized in a person's beliefs and you will know that person's God.[1] Do you
see the importance of belief? Allow me to be even more specific about the
matter.

Your beliefs influence your maturity. We are multifaceted people—
physical beings, intellectual beings, emotional beings, spiritual beings. To
neglect growth in any one facet of our lives is to prevent holistic maturity.
I know some intellectual giants who are emotional Pygmies and some ad-
vanced-age adults who are spiritual infants. Comprehensive growth is essential. Where imbalance is present, life is out of kilter; personhood is
incomplete.

Your beliefs shape your priorities. What you believe determines how
you spend your time, money, and energy; what or whom you will serve;
the object of your greatest allegiance. Why do you want a college education? What will you do with it? Answers to those questions are directly related to the nature of your beliefs. What is most important in life—climbing
to the top in one's profession, making money, finding happiness, experiencing love, serving society? What do you believe?

Your beliefs affect your personal relations. How you treat other people
is determined by what you believe within yourself. Do we have a responsibility related to each other? Can I study in isolation from the needs of the
greater community? Are persons more important than institutions and other
things? What do you believe? The intensity of your belief about these matters will shape your involvement, or lack of it, in community.

Your beliefs determine your actions. Important events are almost always unexplainable apart from a consideration of the beliefs behind them.
We act much more on the basis of what we believe than on the basis of
what we know.

What made Martin Luther King, Jr. act so courageously in the cause
of human equality and social justice? Far more was involved than a concern with the facts. Many people knew the situation, even hated it, but failed
to respond to it. King was moved by what he believed. Thus, he moved
others.

How do you explain a Mother Teresa immersing herself in the rank
poverty and sick squalor of Calcutta? Other people see the starving and

---

[1]Carl E. Braaten, *Stewards of the Mysteries: Sermons for Festivals & Special
Occasions* (Minneapolis: Augsburg Publishing House, 1983) 85.

malnourished, thinly fleshed skeletons on the street. Data about needs are plentiful. Mother Teresa lives as an angel of mercy because of what she believes about people, about God, and about mercy.

What about Bishop Desmond Tutu in South Africa? Why does he respond so adamantly and courageously to the evil atrocity of apartheid? Plenty of people are aware of the problem. Listen to Bishop Tutu's comments to the highly critical judiciously threatening Eloff Commission: "God's purposes are certain. They may remove a Tutu, they may remove the South African Council of Churches, but God's intention to establish his Kingdom of justice, of love, of compassion will not be thwarted. We are not scared, certainly not of the government, or any other perpetrators of injustice and oppression, for victory is ours through Him Who Loved Us!"[2] That is a belief and that belief is the motivation behind Desmond Tutu's action.

Are you beginning to see the importance of the question? Let me tell you why I am raising it with you now. You are beginning a very important segment of your life—a period of concentration on study, dedication to learning, hitting the books. These next few years have been dedicated to intellectual advancement and social development. Good! But, what if belief gets no attention? What if you fail to grow spiritually? Given the nature of our personhood and the reason for our actions, a failure to grow in belief can create a real danger. Beliefs influence our maturity, shape our priorities, affect our personal relations, and determine our actions. Thus, your time in college should include authentic development of the spirit, sound growth in personal belief.

Quite honestly, most of us share precisely the confession of the man in the New Testament story—"I believe, help my unbelief" (Mark 9:24). We believe some things and doubt others. We affirm some matters which are wrong and question other matters which look right. We believe a little and want to believe more or we believe nothing and want to believe something. Our existence embraces both belief and unbelief.

Recently, a man said to me, "I would like to be able to say publicly, 'I don't believe anything' and then privately to begin work on what I do

---

[2]Trevor Huddleston, "Foreword," in Desmond Mpilo Tutu, *Hope and Suffering: Sermons and Speeches,* ed. John Webster (Grand Rapids MI: William B. Eerdmans Publishing Company, 1984) 11.

believe." Where should such a person start? What are the basics of belief? Can we name any minimums?

Here are four suggestions. For me, they are nonnegotiables. Ask me what I believe and I will tell you at least this, probably much more, but at least this. I name these convictions as a means of encouraging your consideration of the beliefs you would name.

A Sense of the Holy. That is where I would start. My belief in God is basic to my belief about anything else or everything else.

Incidentally, my belief in God embraces mystery but is not associated with a disregard for reality. Belief in God does not excuse me from a responsible life in this world. In fact, my most profound experiences with God have been closely related to intimate involvements in society.

Worship is a high priority. Opportunities to nurture our sense of the holy, to express ourselves before God, merit a place of centrality in our lives as individuals and in the activities of this institution. A former Archbishop of Canterbury once said that apart from worship we cannot hope to solve the problems of our world. I agree with that assessment and add to it the observation that apart from worship we cannot hope to negotiate successfully the transitions and crises of our lives. The worship of God is the most primal activity of our personhood.

I start with an affirmation of a sense of the holy.

The Importance of Community. We need each other. Carefully documented experiments have shown that an individual completely isolated from social interchange begins quickly to lose touch with reality. Confusion develops when community disintegrates. That is not surprising. God created us for community.

Community does not require mutual compatibility. I hope you know that. We do not have to be alike and, indeed, we do not have to like each other to have community. Community is grounded in the God who calls us together.

Contributing to the realization of community is a lifelong, worldwide task. We live in an interdependent world. Our learning here or elsewhere cannot be completely unrelated to the larger community—an anxiety-ridden, trigger-happy soldier in Beirut; a fearful diplomat in Moscow; a hungry child in Ethiopia; a beleaguered black woman in Johannesburg. The necessity of community.

The Primacy of Love. The apostle Paul gave us the appropriate tip on this belief a long time ago. Eventually we all get around to an affirmation of it. Listen to Will Durant at age ninety-two. After investing a lifetime in studying and writing about persons and events, this historian-philosopher distilled 2,000 years of history into three simple words, "Love one another." Durant said, "My final lesson of history is the same as that of Jesus. You may think that's a lot of lollipop, but just try it. Love is the most practical thing in the world."[3] Enough said. The primacy of love.

The Necessity of Faith. Søren Kierkegaard was right on target, as usual, when he observed, "What no person has a right to is to delude others into the belief that faith is something of no great significance or that it is an easy matter, whereas it is the greatest and most difficult of things."[4] Now, we have come full circle. To tell you of my basic beliefs is to share with you my conviction about the necessity of faith. I am not talking about blind belief, but about belief with its eyes wide open. True faith does not shut down intellectual inquiry. Rather, a pursuit of truth is an act of faith. Getting an education can be a profound expression of spiritual devotion.

Two people sit in the same classroom, hear the same lectures in political science, and come to understand the system admirably. But, one of these individuals ends up exploiting the system for personal gain and the other serving within the system for social betterment. Why? The difference is a matter of belief. That same principle is involved in an explanation of differences between people's behavioral responses to a knowledge of nuclear power, social structures, and even biblical truths. In the final analysis, action grows out of belief. Thus, true belief is an absolute necessity.

For me, personally, faith makes the most sense in relation to the person called Jesus of Nazareth. My own belief centers on the Christ.

An interesting story has made the rounds in Princeton. One day someone said to Mrs. Einstein, "Do you know all about relativity?" "No," she replied, "but I know my husband and I know he can be trusted."[5] I do not have all the answers regarding questions about life, death, eternity, and the like. In fact, on most days I have as many questions as I do convictions. However, in the person of Christ I have found the revelation of God, a place to put down my faith, the center of my beliefs.

---

[3]Pam Proctor, "Durants on History: From the Ages, With Love," *Parade,* 6 August 1978.

[4]Søren Kierkegaard, *Selections from the Writings of Søren Kierkegaard* (New York: Anchor Books, 1960) 150.

[5]Joseph E. McCabe, *Handel's Messiah: A Devotional Commentary* (Philadelphia: The Westminster Press, 1978) 95.

You will have to determine for yourself where to put your faith. The journey from unbelief to belief must be taken by each one of us individually. I wish I could take it for you. However, I can only promise to support you on it and be a friend throughout it. Please do not delay. Please do not put belief on hold during this experience in academia or at any other time in your life. What you believe is as essential as what you know.

In John Updike's first novel, *The Poor House Fair,* the director of the poor farm has succeeded in destroying the faith upon which several old timers have relied. In an effort to establish his own brand of humanism, the director ruthlessly has disregarded all objections of the older people and sought to eradicate their convictions. Finally, a ninety-four year old pauper school teacher spoke. What he said, we must hear. "Let an old fella say one thing more and then he'll hold his peace. When you get to be my age . . . you shall know this: there is no goodness without belief. There is nothing but busyness. And if you have not believed, at the end of your life you shall know you have buried your talent in the ground of this world and have nothing saved to take into the next."[6]

The stakes are high. The task is crucial. You must answer the question for yourself though I promise to stand with you if there is struggle. What do you believe?

---

[6]Carlyle Marney, *The Carpenter's Son* (Wake Forest NC: Chanticleer Publishing Company, Inc., 1967) 80.

When the Mountain Does Not Move

Mark 11:22-25

G. K. Chesterton once said that Jesus' style was "gigantesque." No better illustration of that truth can be found than Jesus' statement regarding the power of faith. Though some biblical commentators go to great lengths to set the context of this passage precisely on the Mount of Olives overlooking the Dead Sea so that the Lord's reference to a mountain can have specific eschatological meaning, such interpretive antics are unnecessary. Any mountain will do. Jesus was talking theology, not geography. The Master Teacher had picked up a familiar rabbinic phrase and was using it to make a point about faith—a point about the importance of persons possessing the power of faith. We ought to have faith—that is the issue.

Very likely, few, if any, of us would argue with this commendation of faith, this admonition regarding faith. In one way or another, most of us acknowledge the value of faith. However, questions rather than affirmations may greet the validation of faith implied in this particular passage. Jesus' illustration of faith's power presents a problem to us.

Oh, I know that Jesus was not talking about the removal of an actual physical barrier. Just think what life would be like if every individual's personal whim about nature were brought to pass by a simple recognition of faith's presence. What disorder—mountains toppling here and there, valleys filling up and rivers redirected. But, faith does not cause chaos in creation. Actually, the reference of Jesus was to a kind of mountain stronger than a pile of stones and unmovable by mechanical force. However, even if "mountain" is not interpreted literally, the promise remains problematical.

Like you, I am sure, I have listened to numerous moving, inspiring testimonies regarding great transformations affected by faith. Miracles in the present are not mute matters for many persons of faith. To be sure, I am encouraged by these believers.

I know as well individuals for whom apparently faith never has involved any struggle. Quite honestly, I am intimidated by these folks. They always smile—always. When asked how they are doing, they ring out a resilient "great" or "fantastic"—always. Admittedly, maybe the difficulty is with me, but frankly I am suspicious of such people. When facial expressions never change, I begin to wonder if smiles are pasted on, made of plastic, or forced. When a person is always "just super," I consider the strong possibility of superficiality if not artificiality. Authenticity in spirituality does not necessitate jack-o'-lantern-sized smiles and pollyanna expressions of mental attitudes. In reality, too many difficulties exist in our world and far too much tragedy occurs in our lives for a really sensitive individual always to be wearing a smile and feeling great. But, remember, I confess that such critical thoughts may be much more a judgment on myself, an indictment against my faith, than a valid statement about those to whom I have alluded.

Perhaps some people really are immune to difficulties with faith, untouched by periods of doubts, and devoid of demanding spiritual struggles. But, I am not one of those persons and I know that I am not alone. I remember so well on several occasions counseling with a young woman utterly distraught because of her lack of ability to identify with the gospel passage chosen as this sermon's text. With tears trickling down her face she described to me the intensity of her personal faith, the persistence of her prayers regarding a serious problem in her family, and the lack of a realization of any solution for the problem despite a relentless continuation of her faith and prayers. "Is the scripture untrue?" or "Is something wrong with me?" she wanted to know.

Though undoubtedly intended as a comforting admonition for us, these words from Jesus can lead to disconcerting speculation and to disturbing questions within us. What if the mountain does not move? We have faith and we pray, but a major problem persists. Is that difficulty an indication of unrecognized doubt, a sign of some undetected weakness in our faith? Could it be that I am even in worse shape than I know? Does the relentless continuation of a problem represent inadequacies in a person's spiritual condition?

Why does the mountain not move? Maybe that is the better question. At least, this inquiry deserves an answer first. Why does the mountain not move?

Sometimes we simply approach situations with unrealistic expectations. Face the facts. God never promised to people of faith an escape from life, an insulation from difficulties, an immunization against problems. Faith is not some form of magic which when voiced with proper incantations can guarantee immediate solutions to all of life's problems and assure happy endings to every episode of existence. Likewise, faith is not some bargaining chip by which we can obligate God to make our lives trouble free. Possessing faith is not synonymous with putting on rose-colored glasses so that life is completely devoid of any depressing darkness.

Activate your memory. Christianity was born amid tragedy. The very possibility of redemptive faith requires reflections on and confrontations with a cruel, unjust crucifixion. Think through the implications of that truth. To expect faith to be a hedge against difficulties is simply unrealistic. To believe that God shields his people from all problems is naively to cling to a false hope. The combined witness of scriptural truth, historical records, and personal experience is that God provides for his people not an absence of problems but the strength of his presence amid problems, not a detour around difficulties but a way through difficulties.

Alright. We understand faith as a means of encountering life, not escaping from life. Realism is our attitude as we approach difficulties. But still, sometimes the mountain does not move. Now we are not asking why the mountain does not move, but what to do next. What happens when we find no way around, over, under, or through problems? You know the situation, do you not?—a person needs to be forgiven, but forgiveness is buried under a mound of resentment and intentions of retaliation; a bad habit needs to be broken, but every day that habit seems to loom larger than on the day before; a doubt needs to be resolved, but the doubt develops more strength rather than diminishes in strength; a wrong needs to be corrected, but correction seems to involve an insurmountable task; a relational problem needs to be solved, but living with the problem appears less difficult than solving it; an illness needs to be confronted with life-altering adjustments, but the patient is immobilized by pain which will not cease and worry which will not subside; opponents of a cause need to be loved into cooperation, but the effort is too sizable even to be manageable. You know the situation well. What is to happen when the mountain does not move?

"Have faith in God," Jesus said. "I assure you that whoever tells this hill to get up and throw itself in the sea and does not doubt in his heart, but believes that what he says will happen, it will be done for him" (Mark 11:22-23 TEV). I believe the teaching of Jesus. But, what if the hill stays put? What then is to be the posture of belief? Answers to such questions are crucial because here we stand on the edge of defeat tempted toward cynicism. My guess is that precisely right here is where most people live.

Our spiritual brother is the sick boy's father who declared, "I believe; help my unbelief!" (Mark 9:24 RSV)

An experience from the life of Jesus provides insight into our plight in the face of such a predicament. In the Garden of Gethsemane, fatigued by interrogation, hounded by his enemies and frustrated by his friends, Jesus prayed for the removal of a mountain. Remember, "Father, my Father! . . . Take this cup of suffering away from me" (Mark 14:36 TEV). However, no sooner had he finished praying for the removal of a mountain than he got up from his knees and stared into the reality of a life-demanding summit. What did Jesus do? When the mountain did not move for him, what action did he take? Jesus kept on doing exactly what he had been doing.

Apocryphally or actually, one day while hoeing in his garden, St. Francis was approached by a stranger. The passerby inquired what Francis would do if he knew that Christ would come for him that night. Expectations were of frantic preparations in the face of this threat. Reportedly, Francis responded, "I would finish hoeing in my garden, eat my meal, say my prayers, and go to bed."

That is the spirit to which we must aspire. At the very moment when the mountain looms largest—when prayer is unanswered, hope is unrealized, and faith is frustrated—do not give up. Stay on course. Continue in faith.

Actually, it is often at this very point in our pilgrimage that we discover most fully the nature of faith. Faith is found in faithfulness. That is not double talk. Faith for a journey comes on the journey, not in advance of it. Each step of faith leads to additional discoveries of faith which in turn make possible more steps of faith. Such is the economy of faith. Thus, we must go on exercising faith, living faithfully, even when the mountains in our paths are monumental and apparently unmovable.

In truth, if all the evidence must be in hand before faith is exercised, that is not faith. If the future must be filled with certainty before we venture into it, faith is no longer a necessity. Anyone can walk a clearly defined path. Even a person devoid of faith will enter an experience in which security and success are guaranteed. Best understood, faith is a thrust into the future with trust in God—trust in God period, not trust in God if the burden is lifted, the problem is solved, and the mountain is moved. Faith is trust in God.

Recall the interesting Old Testament narrative about the three young Hebrews who were thrown into a furnace because of their devotion to God.

These fiery fellows believed that God would protect them and they claimed as much before the authorities. But, they also indicated they would be faithful to God anyway. Listen, "If the God whom we serve is able to save us from the blazing furnace and from your power, then he will. But even if he doesn't, Your Majesty may be sure that we will not worship your god, and we will not bow down to the gold statue that you have set up" (Daniel 3:17-18 TEV). That is the pattern to be duplicated in our deliberations. We journey affirming a faith that can move mountains but continuing that journey and that faith even if the mountains remain.

Jesus prayed for the removal of the cross from his ministry. Yet, those who ruthlessly would pin him to a tree drew near even as he prayed. Don't forget, though, that Jesus knew the resurrection after the crucifixion and that he knew resurrection only because of crucifixion.

"Does that mean that all will be alright for us if we continue in the faith?" we ask. I do not know. Even that question tempts an evasion of faith—implies a willingness to venture only if there are guarantees. "If I believe in God as he desires, will God provide for me as I desire?" Beware of such bargaining. I really do not know if all will be well for us in the future if we continue in faith. We will not be alone. Our faith will be sufficient either to move mountains or to sustain us as we face the mountains.

I really suspect that much confusion and discouragement among true believers come from a recognition of the plight of other people apart from a perception of the real nature of their pilgrimages. For goodness sake, do not allow some superficial positivist with a fake smile to intimidate you by a whipped-up, counterfeit optimism which is confused with an authentic, toughly developed faith. When we come clean with each other, we understand our common pilgrimages and find encouragement in sharing the same journey.

I very much like the old story of the medieval peasant who one day came face to face with a monk from a much-talked-about monastery. The peasant blurted out impulsively, "Tell me, holy father, what do you men of God do up there in the monastery on the top of the hill? I often look up there and think that that must be the nearest place on earth to heaven. What do you holy men do up there?" Wisely and gently the monk answered, "What do we do up there? I'll tell you, my child. We fall down and we get up. We fall down and we get up. We fall down and we get up."[1]

---

[1]John Claypool, "Keeping the Promise," *Integrity. 1975 Christian Life Commission Seminar Proceedings* (Nashville: The Christian Life Commission of the Southern Baptist Convention, 1975) 65.

So goes life. That is the way it is. We fluctuate between affirming "Lord I believe" and praying "Lord, help my unbelief." We see one mountain removed and another arise. One problem is solved before our eyes but two more now demand attention. Do not be discouraged. No need exists to give up. In faith take heart for the present even as in faith you take hope for the future. Journey on with courage. Faith is sufficient for the hour. The faith that removes mountains or takes people through mountains has the potential to sustain us if the mountain does not move, to strengthen us at the foot of the mountain until the way of the future is revealed—whether or not that way is flat or mountainous. Such is the much-welcomed realization encouraged by the good news of our faith in Jesus Christ.

A Fight to the Start

Jacob is my brother and his crossing point along the Jabbok River is my home. Not literally, of course. But spiritually that is the sense of the matter. What happened to that traveler there happens to this preacher here. And, no doubt, the same is true for you to some extent.

Consider the biblical narrative regarding Jacob, possible points of personal identification with it, and some of the enduring truths regarding the life of faith which come from it.

Sundown and solitude. Undoubtedly, the comments described the condition of Jacob's soul as well as the fading light on the horizon and the lack of fellowship in his camp. The situation was right for introspection at best, if not conducive to depression at worst.

Jacob had acted like a scoundrel. He knew it just as others did. Jacob's sins are not my sins, but there are enough for all of us. Each of us is all too familiar with darkness—across the land and within our lives. Though solitude is often sought, undesired solitude strikes us as a threat. Quietness beats against the eardrums of our spirits like blaring sirens.

Precisely what we have feared most happens first. A struggle begins. For a fleeting moment we may think that we are fighting with our peers—the opponents are honest enemies. Then, we come to suspect a civil turmoil—a battle raging within ourselves. Finally, though, we come clean within our consciences and admit that the struggle is with God.

Doubts, questions, and disturbing thoughts repressed amid full agendas in the presence of various crowds suddenly surface forcefully when we are alone. First, of ourselves we inquire: What is going on with me? Have I been victimized by my culture? Did my parents err in my potty training? Could it be that I am truly a sinner? Why am I like this, Lord? Speaking of "Lord," we turn directly to our momentary adversary: Why are you here? Have you come to judge me? Will you speak words of a blessing or of a curse?

Before any divine response can be voiced, we lay into the Almighty. "I will show you Sovereign God!" "There is a lot wrong with this world.

You need to own up to it. Though you may think I am playing a bit dirty, I want to know why innocent people suffer, why tragedies are no respecters of persons and why sincere prayers go unanswered.'' Reeling off our list of charges almost breathlessly—we are on a roll—we think for a split second, ''I've got him. He cannot handle this. I am winning. Victory is mine.'' Then comes the rest of the second and a surge of sickness—''But, if I have whipped God, then he is not God, there is no God, and I am left helpless and alone in this world!''

Almost mesmerized, if not paralyzed, by our thoughts, suddenly a blow staggers us, jars us to full alertness, hurts us. For Jacob, the pain was in his hip. For us, hurt may reside in the mind or in the heart or in the spirit. Perhaps, as in the case of this Jewish forebear, a bone is out of joint. But, of course, it could be that all of life is amiss, unconnected.

Though wounded, Jacob is not defeated. We do not quit this task quickly or easily. The stakes are too high—faith, loyalty, trust, devotion. Already in his earlier days, Jacob had tricked his father and gained a blessing. Maybe now he could do a similar number on God. At least he would not let go of God until he had received a blessing from God. We tend to hang on too.

To be perfectly honest, the nature of my struggle is not precisely the same as that of Jacob's battle. Most often I grapple to get exactly what I want—a life that is easy, problems which always are solved, every question answered, challenges without difficulties, only acquaintances who are nice, and an absence of ambiguity with the omnipresence of simplicity. My way of doing things would involve mistakes with no bad consequences, repentance without pain, and forgiveness with no cost. Why can't God see the wisdom of all of that?

Oh, at my best moments I know that my struggle is fiercest with the very one who loves me most. So often such is the case. Within love we are honest—even disgustingly honest. I want faith on my terms. I desire a god shaped by my expectations. So, I commit myself to wrestle with this holy night visitor, to grapple with this intruding Deity. By the Jabbok River or anywhere else, let him come. I am fit for a fight to the finish.

To be sure, eventually, though, it takes some of us much longer than one night to get the point. But truth does eventually emerge with the inbreaking light of some new dawn. As the playwright has suggested, our arms are indeed too short to box with God. Ultimately, faith must be on his terms, not mine. Only when I let go of trying to run heaven and earth do I discover that, so long as I desire him, God never will let go of me—

on earth or in heaven. Surrender—that act which has seemed so much like a weak-kneed throwing-in of the towel— surrender strangely comes to be seen as strength. Winning is in fact in losing when the fight is with God. The struggle ceases.

Catching a deep breath, which seems like new wind, we walk away from the sight of the most recent wrestling match. Bruises from the struggle remain, but a sense of healing prevails. As we are walking we notice that we are limping a bit. So be it. The sun is rising.

Now, please note two or three observations about enduring truths of the life of faith incorporated in these narratives. First,

Conflict Is Inevitable

Predictably, people respond to God with both anger and compassion. We long to be drawn toward God and we seek to run from God. Even after years of searching for God, periodically we attempt to go in hiding from God. Conflict is inevitable.

Redemption comes as a gift and a demand. Freedom and responsibility are intertwined. Salvation involves incredible joy and heavy duty. While we celebrate the blessings of God which are upon us, we protest the accompanying expectations of God which are set before us. We accept divine gifts happily and argue about divine requests vigorously.

God's love is as demanding as it is enriching. An invitation to Christian discipleship promises the highest quality of life possible but tolerates no compromises and allows no rivals. Life with God is an all-or-nothing matter. God extends grace to us but expects us in return to love him completely and not to fool around with any higher loyalty. Jesus blessed those who pursued good for righteousness' sake and praised those who were persecuted for his sake. We stop short. It is a mixed bag. Frankly, we like the possibility of goodness but resist any risk of persecution.

At times God appears as enemy rather than friend, as disrupter instead of Savior, as rival not Redeemer. Study the biblical story. More than once those who have been most in love with God have been locked into the most vicious struggles with God. Conflict is inevitable. Second,

Struggle Is Essential

Dostoyevsky's tale of the Grand Inquisitor is far too true and personal to rank as enjoyable reading. No sooner has Christ entered our lives than we want him out of our lives. While we enjoyed a relationship with Christ in the past, we do not want too much of Christ in the present. Commitment to Christ creates peace internally but often elicits conflict externally. Devotion to Christ causes disruption in relation to others. Strangely Dostoyevsky's cardinal inquisitor speaks precisely our sentiments in relation to Jesus' involvement with us today, "Go and come no more. Come not at all, never, never!"[1]

For whatever reasons, most of us seek to negotiate the nonnegotiable, to purchase at our price that which is not for sale at any price. We like glory but not commitment. We revel in expressions of grace for ourselves but devilishly demand other means for relating to others. Thus, we cord off a ring by some river called Jabbok, in some school called Mercer, or at some other place along our path, and we go at it with God.

Admittedly, not all people do faith this way. Some persons can turn off their minds and hearts completely, feign passivity as a form of piety, and boisterously claim absolutely no disruptions along their spiritual pilgrimages. Their smug smiles make me sick. Oh, I must admit that in moments of weakness and fatigue, I find myself wishing I could do it that way. Certainly it looks easier. However, I know better.

Struggle simply cannot be discounted as an important dimension of the life of faith. Show me a faith which never has known struggles and I will show you a faith gained by proxy, inherited by family; a faith marked by superficiality.

Only a faith for which we have fought is a faith which can sustain us in any fight. That faith over which we have lost sleep, about which we have engaged life's ultimate issues is the faith that saves and sustains. A faith which has not known struggle like a faith fearful of struggle is not the faith of either Jacob or of Jesus. Struggle is essential. Third,

A Resolution in Faith Is Possible

Look carefully. Jacob walked away from the River Jabbok with a limp. But, the man did walk away, and in faith. Note carefully where he went, almost immediately—to meet his brother and to redress old wrongs. Finally, Jacob had found a faith in God which changed the entirety of his life.

---

[1]Fyodor Dostoyevsky, *The Grand Inquisitor* (New York: Frederick Ungar Publishing Co., 1969) 22.

We—you and I—can know such faith. No promise exists that we can know it apart from struggle. But, we can know such faith.

Conflict is inevitable. Struggle is essential. But, a resolution in faith is possible. Nikos Kazantzakis makes the point superbly in his book *Report to Graeco*. A young truth seeker went to a monastic community off the coast of Greece. He wanted to visit with the hermits there and to discover their way to God. One day he talked with an old hermit who had lived alone for forty years. The young man asked his spiritual father if he struggled with the devil. Immediately the old man responded negatively explaining that his flesh was too old for that. He went on to say that his struggle now was with God. The young man was astonished. Incredulously he pondered a struggle with God and then asked his elder if he hoped to win. The old man immediately dismissed that idea completely and indicated that he hoped to lose.

As Jacob walked away from Jabbok ford a new day was dawning—across the land and in his heart. Jacob limped noticeably but he walked confidently in faith—a secure faith fit for any struggle because it was a faith born in struggle.

Please do not miss the truth involved. After a serious grappling with God there is a future. Maybe there is a real future only after grappling with God. To pursue an honest faith in God is to commit oneself to a fight to the start—to a struggle which leads to surrender, to a wrestling match with the Redeemer which results in a faith which makes possible a new creation.

Do you dare?

Take Her Off the Moon!

Luke 1:46-55; John 1:14

Recently I have spent a considerable amount of time trying to take seriously the advice given by Robert McAfee Brown in his delightfully disturbing volume entitled *Unexpected News*.[1] As a result, as best I could, I have tried to listen to the gospel with different ears, to see its truth with new eyes, and to consider its meaning from an unfamiliar perspective. Quite honestly, I have not been totally successful.

Brown has made a sound case for turning to the gospel with the mentality of a citizen in a third-world nation and from that base studying the gospel as if it never had been read before. Though I have traveled a good bit in third-world nations and dialogued as well as worshiped with believers in them, I have not found this new discipline without difficulty. At points, I have bristled defensively. At other points, I have sensed an impulse to react negatively. Open-minded theology and Bible study is one thing, but when lifestyles are threatened by it, that is something else! I want to write off some of what I have read as sheer radicalism. But, I cannot escape the fact that I have been reading the gospel—*the* gospel.

Well, I am not through with all of that. Though I would like to set it aside, I cannot quite do it. Even if I do not have the courage to embody the truth, I am not cowardly enough to set truth aside. Maybe the gnawing guilt of dealing with it but not doing anything about it is an easier plight than living with the consequences of a truly incarnational life. I do not think that is the case with me, but I would not rule out completely that possibility. I just do not want to turn loose of a potentially life-altering approach to the gospel until both that gospel and that approach get a firm hold on me.

So much for the confession. Let me tell you why I mention it in a sermon. Dealing with biblical texts from the point of view of the dispossessed

---

[1]Robert McAfee Brown, *Unexpected News. Reading the Bible with Third World Eyes* (Philadelphia: The Westminster Press, 1984).

has reinforced within me some conclusions which relate directly to our life together.

In one South American country, a number of priests conduct Sunday services in which the people present comment on the events of the week and interact with the priest and with each other regarding selected passages of Scripture. Please hear a description and a partial transcript of one such session.

The presiding priest began with an observation and a question. "Today is September 12. Does that date mean anything special to you?" A parishioner responded, "Three years ago today Allende was killed in Chili and the Chileans lost their leader. Now they are suffering repression." Another person mentioned the death of Martin Luther King, Jr., explaining that both of the men named were concerned about oppressed people. The priest then asked, "Doesn't the day mean anything but *death* to you?" That provoked this comment, "Well, today is also the Feast of the Holy Name of Mary. So this day makes me think of her." When the priest inquired as to whether or not any connection existed between Allende, Martin Luther King, Jr., and Mary, the parishioner said that the answer depended on whether or not Mary was concerned about oppressed people. At that point, the priest read the opening verses from Mary's song, "The Magnificat," recorded in Luke's gospel.

No sooner had the priest completed the Scripture reading than someone shouted, "Bravo! But, Father, that doesn't sound at all like the Mary we hear about in the cathedral. And the Mary in the 'Holy Pictures' certainly doesn't look like a person who would talk that way." Surely, sometime you have seen those gaudy religious pictures done in a cheap baroque of bright colors and syrupy profiles and surrounded with lace upon lace. The priest asked about the Mary of the pictures. One person who had such a picture in his possession held it up for all to see and commented, "Here she is. She is standing on a crescent moon. She is wearing a crown. She has rings on her fingers. She has a blue robe embroidered with gold." "That does sound like a different Mary from the Mary of the song," the priest commented, and then asked, "Do you think the picture has betrayed the Mary of the song?"

One individual said, "The Mary who said that God 'has exalted those of low degree' would not have left all of her friends so she could stand on the moon." All at once several people shouted, "Take her off the moon!" What followed was an intriguing litany of individual comments and corporate shouts:

"The Mary who said that God 'has put down the mighty from their thrones,' would not be wearing a crown."

"Take off her crown!" the people shouted.

"The Mary who said that God 'had sent the rich empty away' would not be wearing rings on her fingers."

"Take off her rings!"

"The Mary who said that God 'has filled the hungry with good things' would not have left people who were still hungry to wear a silk robe embroidered with gold."

"Take off her robe!"

Someone, struck with embarrassment, suddenly blurted out, "But, Father, this is not right! We're—we're doing a striptease of the Virgin." The priest commented, "Very well. If you don't like the way Mary looks in this picture, what do you think the Mary of the song would look like?" Listen to the responses:

"The Mary of the song would not be standing on the moon. She would be standing in the dirt and dust where we stand."

"The Mary of the song would not be wearing a crown. She would have on an old hat like the rest of us, to keep the sun from causing her to faint."

"The Mary of the song would not be wearing jeweled rings on her fingers. She would have rough hands like ours."

"The Mary of the song would not be wearing a silk robe embroidered with gold. She would be wearing old clothes like the rest of us."

"Father, it may be awful to say this, but it sounds as though Mary would look just like me! My feet are dirty, my hat is old, my hands are rough, and my clothes are torn."

"I think she would be more at home here in the slum with us than in the cathedral or the General's Mansion."[2]

"Take her off the moon!" The shout has kept on resounding in my ears and reverberating through my heart. Mary is only a prototype, of course, a case in point. At stake in this dialogue is the status of all biblical characters—even the nature of God. What have we done? Have we not taken a rough-edged piece of radically good news uncontainable in any culture and sought to sandpaper off the edges so as to make it palatable in our place of residence and beautiful as an affirmation of our styles of life? To be believable must God be white, middle class, and documentably suc-

---

[2]Brown, *Unexpected News*, 85-88.

cessful? If not, at least we can reason that God is unconcerned about color, status, and success. Even those Sunday School pictures which we know suggest that Jesus and the rest of those biblical people were very different from us and have little to say to us. In those familiar posterboard scenes, halos were prominent, rainbows filled backgrounds, skies were cloudless, robes never had rips or stains, sandal-shod feet were immaculately clean, and no sweat could be found on faces emblazoned by a white hot sun. Even depictions of the crucifixion were neat. If that *is* the way it *was,* that *is not* the way it *is*. So, we see little connection between the two worlds and their inhabitants. The matter is either one of irrelevance—no connection between the two worlds—or of distance—God and his kind are above all of this stuff in which we live.

"Take her off the moon" jars us out of all of that, forces us to see the biblical message in relation to contemporary reality. High-gloss generalizations must give way to dull, gory details. The gospel is about the *word become flesh*—God with us, Jesus in our midst, redemption in our lives, discipleship in this world! If you try to live it another way or to put it all somewhere above this life, out of touch, for God's sake and for the world's sake, come off it.

Two convictions have been reconfirmed for me.

One, the gospel is for this world. God chose to do his greatest work in our midst. If a concentration on the gospel creates distance between this world and us, we best recheck our sources. Likely we either have looked at the wrong gospel or we have misinterpreted it. The word became *flesh*. God revealed himself in this world.

Actually we cannot be too specific about the truth involved. In the birth of Jesus, God identified himself with the very kind of family we refer to Family Services, to the Salvation Army, or to some other community agency. Jesus associated with and even praised people like those whom we criticize and hurriedly cart off to get cleaned up, fed, and made more socially acceptable. Forgiveness was a way of life which Jesus lived, not just a word he said. Forgiveness was to be a manner of relating on this earth, not just a manner of getting someone to heaven. As a result of Christ's forgiveness, a radical insurrectionist could share a meal and fellowship with a rabid nationalist. Today, the forgiveness of Christ requires reconciliation between people who do not even desire conversation.

And, grace. Look at this matter of grace carefully. Far from a heavenly commodity, or just some neat text which can be set to a nice tune musically, Jesus intended grace to be a present reality—grace which would set a prisoner free, grace which would say to a person caught in the very act of adultery, ''Be going, get on with your life.'' Notice the stark absence of those comments which claim a loud dominance in our lives. Where is the judgment? Where is the reprimand? Are there no standards? Jesus lived as he taught by a radical grace— grace not as a generality, but grace as a specific way of life; a grace that got tired, dirty, dumped on, besieged, abused, and embraced.

My fear is that we have so spiritualized much of what Jesus said that we may have distorted it beyond recognition. The joy of the sermon on the plain was intended for today, not some distant tomorrow. Jesus said, ''Blessed are you poor'' (Luke 6:20 RSV). We quickly add the comforting explanation that surely he must have meant the ''poor in spirit.'' We tend to do a similar injustice to his beatitude about making peace. Jesus identified himself—really identified himself—with hungry, thirsty, lonely, and imprisoned people. We satisfy ourselves with the assurance that his words are only figurative. Ironically, even some of the most avid biblical literalists explain that obviously such a passage cannot be taken literally.

The gospel is for this world! A plea accompanies this statement of my conviction. Let us quit tampering with the gospel, stop making the relevant irrelevant, desist from divorcing from life that which pulsates with life, refrain from refusing to recognize the earthy nature of the incarnation. Jesus was no sweet, otherworldly phantom flitting about Palestine flippantly spouting off memorable phrases and serendipitously doing nice things. Jesus was a dark-skinned Jewish man, racked by temptations and hounded by critics, who did his Father's will despite the cost. Jesus lived where people partied, suffered where they worshiped, and died where they dumped their garbage. The God revealed by Jesus is a God for us in this world. This God is as much at home in a prison as in a prayer room. Almighty God of the ages does not shrink back from persons temporarily plagued by doubts, harassed by family difficulties, or defeated by unemployment. God is as fit for the cancer ward as for the cathedral. The gospel is for *this* world.

Second, persons who are servants of the gospel live responsibly in society. Obeying God and following Christ mean living helpfully and redemptively in society—making a difference for good where we are.

As God's people, we cannot hide, lose ourselves in the books, and construct ivory towers conducive to confinement. What we read, study, think, and learn must interact with all that is going on around us. Christians know no interim for inactivity. Talking cannot be made a substitute for acting. Thinking about solutions to problems will not suffice for efforts aimed at solving problems. We must not study economics, history, and literature blind to the contemporary currents of violence, poverty, and injustice which rush through our world. We dare not affirm the barrier-eradicating love of God and continue nurturing cliques, never breaking out of narrowly defined group loyalties.

"What is wrong with you?" you may ask. "This message seems radical, perhaps even scandalous, surely not positive enough and sufficiently supportive for us to feel better." Honestly, such radicality comes with the territory when the turf traversed is the truth of scripture. Scandal is inherent in the gospel. No one has to whip it up or tack it on.

My concern is a simple one— that we hear the gospel for what it is, God's word for this world, and that as servants of God we begin to live out the gospel in this world—not tomorrow but today. When I falter in these regards or fail, as I do regularly, I try to remember words which I now commend to your memories.

From a group of anonymous prophets in South America: "Take her off the moon!" "Take her off the moon!"

From a philosopher-theologian published in the Fourth Gospel of the New Testament: "The Word became flesh (a human being) and dwelt among us" (John 1:14).

From the Lord of history, the Savior of the world, Jesus himself: "as you did it to one of the least of these . . . you did it to me" (Matthew 25:40).

Repentance and Joy

Repent! We cannot seem to get away from that word— displayed on the bumper sticker of an old, faded green, beat-up Volkswagen Beetle; scrawled across a fence with spray paint; crudely posted by the roadway on a weatherworn signboard made to look like a cross. Occasionally some-one finds an unwashed eighteen-wheeler truck and with imaginative, evangelistic zeal swipes away at its big backside until the clean strokes spell "Repent." Numerous television shepherds waving clenched fists and call-ing for offerings scream the term across the air waves and into the ears of their electronically created sheep. Now we cannot even go to a ball game and get away from it. Someone wears the word on a T-shirt or tacks it up as a banner. Thus, down in some end zone alongside "Beat 'em up"; "Kill"; "Win"; and other cute sayings, we see a poster board which reads "Repent!" Oh yes, the words also can be found in the Bible. We cannot consider large segments of the Scriptures or hear extended commentary on them and not be confronted by "repent." We cannot seem to get away from that word.

How do you hear it, or read it—repent? What kinds of images does the word conjure up in your mind? What is the tone?

For most of my life, the word has carried a rather harsh connotation and prompted negative associations. "Repent!" is a scathing command by a solemn-faced, if not angry-looking, person who is pointing a long, slen-der finger in my face—or, at least, so I imagined. Hearing the word has often given me the feeling of being boxed in, trapped. Just the declaration of the word seems to be a condemnation of any hearer of it. When I am addressed by it, invariably, I feel guilty—guilty to the point of even want-ing to confess sins that I have not committed, though God knows I have committed far too many.

Surely if we need to write the word "repent" we should do it in red ink and follow it with an exclamation point or maybe, better still, expand it: "Repent now." "Repent before you die." "Repent or perish." Read or heard, the word repent makes us squirm. Talk about repentance qualifies as bad news.

Unfortunately, knowing the meaning of repentance did little to aid my understanding of its positive nature. Taken from the Greek word *metanoia,* fundamentally repentance means "to change"—to change directions, to turn around, to move toward a new goal, to alter affections, to seek a different destination. Within a specifically Christian context, repentance involves a decision and subsequent action to cease walking away from God. All of life is changed. Conversion occurs.

An individual who is commanded to repent is encouraged to recognize that something is bad wrong in life, that life is out of kilter and needs to be changed. To repent is to make the needed change, to allow life to be altered. However, for me, even that decision and action seemed to be heavy, frightful, fitful, and difficult.

Only recently I have come to realize the intimate association between repentance and joy—that is right, repentance and *joy.* Previously I did not think joy was within one hundred miles of repentance. But I was wrong, very wrong. In fact, today I do not know how I missed for so long the essential truth at stake here. Nowhere clearer than in Luke 15, the joy of repentance is a recurring theme throughout the gospels. And, not all of the joy is in heaven. A person who repents experiences joy. Repentance and joy go hand in hand. Joy pervades repentance. Repentance leads to more joy. I regret I had not seen it sooner. My guess is that I am not the only one who has missed that truth. What about you?

One problem is that, in our understanding of Christian conversion, we attempt to start where the New Testament always ends. In much contemporary preaching and teaching, repent is the first word sounded. In New Testament preaching and teaching, repent was the last word sounded. Look at the ministry of Jesus. When the Lord began his public ministry, he announced, "The time is fulfilled, and the Kingdom of God is at hand" and then, *and then*—after that announcement—he said, "Repent" (Mark 1:15). A similar pattern is discernible in the preaching of the early church. Typically, in apostolic preaching, salvation history was reviewed, Jesus was presented as the fulfillment of ancient promises, the exaltation of Jesus and the presence of the Holy Spirit were acclaimed, the imminent end of history was predicted, and then, *and then,* the need for repentance was declared.

Biblically, the call to repentance always follows the announcement of good news. An imperative from God is always preceded by an indicative from God. Such an order makes sense pragmatically as well as theologically. To demand that an individual change without any offer of power by which the change can be made is cruel. Repentance without the gospel is bad news. If a call to repentance comes first, how are we ever to obey it? Must we lift ourselves by our own bootstraps? Do we need to whip up enough strength to change ourselves before we can come before God?

When "repent" is always the first word of Christian preaching or the only word in Christian preaching, there is no joy. We are left to believe that God will love us only if we can straighten out ourselves enough to be lovable; that God will grant us salvation only if we can work on ourselves sufficiently so as to seem to deserve it. In such a situation, repentance is a work of human achievement, the product of personal efforts.

We simply must hear again the New Testament message and see clearly the New Testament order of things. The possibility of repentance is related to the availability of God's grace—and God's grace is a given. We do not have to work for it, earn it, justify it, or merit it. We are acceptable to God now! We are loved by God today! In no sense must we rely on our own strength, pick ourselves up, turn ourselves around. That is the work of God in us. All we need to do is to allow God to do all he wants to do in us and through us.

All of us want to be loved by God, acceptable to God. Furthermore, when we see what God is doing in our world, we want to be a part of it. We seek such love, power, mercy, and mission. In response to our desire to be a part of God's work, to be beneficiaries of God's grace, we are told that what we want is precisely what God has in store for us. Then, we are told to repent. Repentance is the mode of entry into God's mission, the doorway to divine power, the means by which we are made to know God's mercy, love, and grace. Thus, repentance is a privilege, a joy, which we are eager to experience.

Once the true nature of repentance is realized, calls for repentance can be recognized as promises not threats, as summons to joyful opportunities not sirens of doleful responsibilities.

We read of lives being changed radically. We hear about people in whom fulfillment has replaced meaninglessness, hope has dispelled despair. We want that for ourselves—want it desperately. Can we have it? Yes. How? By way of repentance.

"I am wrung out. Life seems to be over although I thought it had just begun. Now there is a terrible treadmill. I run and run and get nowhere and grow weary. I want to live abundantly. I need help. What must I do?'' Repent!

"I am caught up in a cycle of evil. One wrong act precipitates other wrong acts. Sinning is as easy as scooting down a slick slide. My situation is worsening. I am growing more and more desperate. For me, life is being destroyed. I want out. I want to do better. Is there any hope?'' Yes. "What should I do?'' Repent!

"Actually nobody knows me. I can cover things up pretty well, make even something wrong look right. Yet, the cheating and lying now seem like a slow form of dying. How can I be honest again? How can I come clean?'' Repent!

"Hatred is eating away at my innards. I stagger under the weight of a desire for retaliation. A bent toward violence rips at my soul. How can I change? What am I to do?'' Repent!

Do you hear? In every instance, repentance is not a weight to be carried but a way to be liberated. Repentance is an avenue along which we can move from despair to hope, from frustration to fulfillment, from meaninglessness to purpose, from loneliness to love. Of course, cost is involved. But the joy to be received almost obliterates the cost to be paid, certainly renders it inconsequential. What we move to in repentance is so much more than what we leave behind!

Perhaps in the distant past repentance was a negative act devoid of joy— a turning to the heavy burden of the law, reaching out to a dismally dry ritual, accepting the imposition of a religious system designed to provoke more guilt. If so, no more. In light of the revelation of Christ, the declaration "repent" is received as an invitation to happiness.

Repentance is turning to someone who loves you more than anyone else loves you, even more than you love yourself. Repentance is accepting a future filled with grace. Repentance is opting to live by love. Repentance is engaging tomorrow with hope. Repentance is accepting forgiveness. Repentance is removing guilt.

Interestingly, repentance is not nearly so concerned with the past as with the future. Turning is involved, but it is more of a turning to than a turning from. Thus repentance need not be a lip-biting, teeth-gritting, gut-wrenching act. Hear the gospel. Repentance is a flight to freedom, a human response to the R.S.V.P. on God's invitation to joy.

Do you see? Regardless of your condition, no matter what your sin, that is the promise of repentance. No wonder Clarence Jordan said that repentance does not have even one tiny little bit of sorrow in it and that the happiest, most joyful thing we will ever do is to repent.

An analogy from Jordan makes the point of the sermon beautifully. A caterpillar is a fit little creature for a season. But caterpillars have no business trying to exist in the spring. They simply are not made for it. Thus, at the changing of the seasons, with the inbreaking of a new order of nature, caterpillars are changed. Skins are split apart and from the bodies of caterpillars come butterflies—creatures equipped to glide on the breezes of spring and to live by the nectar of new flowers. What happens to caterpillars is a metamorphosis.

In a very real sense, *metanoia* is like metamorphosis. Repentance facilitates changes which make us fit for life in a new order—the Kingdom of God. Would you say to a caterpillar in some springtime, ''I am so sorry that you have to become a butterfly''? Would you expect the caterpillar to weep and to mourn because of the possibilities of flight? Of course not. Likewise, sorrow has no part in that repentance which contains the promise of life in the Kingdom of God. We accept the change readily, enthusiastically. *Metanoia* is as good for us as metamorphosis is for caterpillars.[1]

Whatever your sin, whatever the condition of your heart, hear the message of Jesus. No finger is pointed in your face; rather hands and arms are outstretched in welcome. Smiles not scowls cover the Master's face. His declaration before you really is an invitation to you— to all of us. Here is the final word of the good news which is the first word of a good life. Hear it well. The end is joy. ''The time is fulfilled, and the kingdom of God is at hand; repent, and believe in the gospel'' (Mark 1:15).

---

[1]Clarence Jordan, *The Substance of Faith and Other Cotton Patch Sermons,* ed. Dallas Lee (New York: Association Press, 1972) 94.

On Forgiveness

Matthew 18:21-22; 6:12-15

Accepting the forgiveness of God is a snap compared with practicing for-giveness in relation to others. You know what I mean. Just think of the explosive anger engendered by the actions of a former friend, the relent-less hurt stoked by thoughts of an estranged lover, the endless pain pro-voked by the betrayal of a marital partner, the deep hostility directed toward a colleague with whom you have been in conflict. Receiving forgiveness from God is easy. Extending forgiveness to others is difficult. Yet, ac-, cording to the New Testament, a direct relationship exists between the two. In the little epistle of James we are told that God will deal with us after the manner in which we deal with others. A memorable parable in the gospels makes the point that being forgiven and extending forgiveness belong to-gether. Jesus even taught us to pray that God would treat our trespasses against him in the same way that we treat people who trespass against us. A very dangerous prayer! Do we really want God to forgive us in direct proportion to our forgiveness of others?

When you think about it, you can understand our hesitancy related to forgiveness. After all, most of us maintain a strong sense of fairness. What is fair—that wrong be punished, that one who does wrong get what is com-ing to him or her? "This woman told a scandalous lie about me. Why should she not be victimized by the same evil? It seems good enough for her." "So what if the man gets hurt? He hurt me." Many people continue to hold to the old Hebraic conviction regarding an eye for an eye and a tooth for a tooth. It seems fair. To offer forgiveness in the face of wrongdoing appears to be unfair, letting the wrongdoer off too easily. Let fairness rule.

Then too, revenge can be disguised to look like justice. Getting even personally can be construed as doing right morally. "To each his due"—that is justice classically defined. You know what our retaliatory minds do with this ancient concept. We make it a justification for getting back. "He did me so dirty. He violated my confidence and betrayed my trust. He does not deserve forgiveness. All the bad that comes to him is justified." Even in perpetrating a vengeful hurt, we pass ourselves off as administrators of justice.

Of course, the fact is that in our world forgiveness is made to seem weak. Grace is for the powerless. The really strong fight back. One who is forgiving comes off looking like "Caspar Milquetoast," a "pushover," a person who is naive and easy. Preeminent in our macho society are the attitudes: "You can't push me around and get away with it." "You can't do me wrong and escape paying for it." Strength and power are measured in force, not expressed through forgiveness.

Let's face it. Forgiveness does not get good press. The act is even more difficult to embrace than the idea is to swallow. Yet, the manner in which we forgive others establishes the pattern by which God forgives us. Besides, our spiritual health is adversely affected when forgiveness is not extended. Think what happens. Unrelieved hatred, resilient resentment, and a passionate desire for retaliation eat away at our innards, destroy the very core of our beings. Ironically, the object of the anger and hostility is totally unaffected. We alone are hurt. I have seen persons literally devastated— physically and emotionally as well as spiritually—by a refusal to practice forgiveness.

Jesus knew full well the destructive power of unrelieved resentment and the constructive force of genuine forgiveness. Thus, he commended forgiveness without conditions. When questioned by his disciples as to how often forgiveness should be extended, Jesus responded with a number intended to suggest as often as it is needed. Health within oneself and a proper relationship with God are both dependent upon the practice of forgiveness in association with others. George Herbert stated the matter succinctly, "He that cannot forgive others breaks the bridge over which he himself must pass if he would reach heaven; for everyone has need to be forgiven."[1]

Alright. Extending forgiveness to others is as essential as receiving forgiveness from God. But how do you do it? How does forgiveness come about? How can I practice forgiveness in relation to other people?

Well, *you start with memory*. That is right— with memory. "Forgive and forget" may be attractive catch words but they do not constitute accurate advice. Actually, forgetting is a hindrance to forgiving. If you forget, you will never forgive. The route to forgiveness does not run through

---

[1]David W. Augsburger, *Seventy Times Seven. The Freedom of Forgiveness* (Chicago: Moody Press, 1970) 15.

a denial of hurt, an escape from pain, or a retreat into fantasy about the absence of wrongdoing—all forms of forgetfulness.

Evil cannot be dealt with seriously until it is accepted realistically. Only realists are forgivers. God offers a good model. Never does God act as if we have done no wrong. Constantly he bears the full brunt of our immorality. The cross represents God squarely facing into our sins. The possibility of divine forgiveness is extended to us amid the reality of our sinfulness.

A realistic look at a broken relationship usually involves a recognition, if not a confession, of self wrong. Seldom are we merely sinned against. Rarely are problems one-sided. Remembering a specific wrong involves acknowledging our involvement in it, admitting that we are a part of the difficulty that is now causing hostility. Thus, the gap between us and the one at whom we are angry is narrowed considerably. We know that wrongdoing exists on both sides. Instead of placing blame on someone else, we act to accept our own responsibility.

The true test of forgiveness is not the removal of an event from our memory but an eradication of bitterness, a lessening of the pain. A wound is recalled but no longer is there any poison in it. We have the ability to forgive what we remember.

You start with memory. Then, *you allow the power of love to do its work*. You care. You care greatly. The lowest point of morality comes in the confession, "I could not care less." Forgiveness is not indicative of a lack of care but expressive of immense care.

Minimally you value the other person as an individual of dignity and worth. Such qualities are results of God's gifts. God values every person, so we value each other. Even one who has wronged us has retained worth. We acknowledge that worth.

Eventually we move toward love. We develop the ability to separate persons from their actions, to distinguish between individuals and their deeds. We may totally despise a particular action but continue to respect and even love the person behind it.

Most likely we will have difficulty in coming to such a conviction about others unless we experience compassion in relation to ourselves. As we understand our own worth undestroyed by our evil actions, we comprehend the worth of others. Self-love becomes an impetus in our love for others. We love even those who have done wrong to us. We love them not because of what they have done or because of what they can do but because of who they are.

As a result of an operative love we do not act to intensify the other person's sense of sin or to increase guilt. Our goal is not to establish a one-upmanship in which we place the other person in our debt. In fact, we do not desire release for ourselves at the expense of another's suffering. Thus, we act in love even toward the one who has offended us and we extend forgiveness.

Finally, *you perform spiritual surgery by editing your memory.* You refuse to allow the past to control the present. You do not permit someone else's behavior to determine your attitude and action.

A kind of repentance occurs. You turn around. You stop directing your attention to the past and begin focusing on the future. You cease facing the reality of the evil and turn to facing the possibility of good.

Do not be mistaken. It is not as easy as it sounds. David Augsburger acknowledged the difficulty when he wrote that "Resentment is a bulldog bite that clinches the teeth of memory into the dead past and refuses to let go."[2] Many people prefer to cling to their pain, grief, and anger than to turn loose of them. Some favor a love-hate relationship with the offending party rather than outright forgiveness.

Essential to forgiveness is a radical turning from the past. That is the only way you can alter the present and change the future. You release people from their pasts. Such an act is distinctly different from excusing a person of an evil deed or deciding to tolerate what has been done. In forgiveness you turn toward the future. Lewis Smedes calls it the most creative act of which human beings are capable.[3] In forgiveness we create a new beginning out of past pain. In turn we experience a new freedom. Several writers have summarized the act of forgiveness in this manner—it is letting what was, be gone; what will be, come; and what is now, be.

Our forgiveness before God is directly related to, dependent upon, our forgiveness in relation to each other. Think of that truth and you begin to sense the importance of the idea and the urgency of the act. Forgiveness is a prerequisite for living healthily and dying redemptively.

Most always I am deeply moved by Howard Thurman's stories. One on forgiveness stands out in my mind.

---

[2]David W. Augsburger, *Caring Enough to Forgive. True Forgiveness* (Scottdale PA: Herald Press, 1981) 50.

[3]Lewis B. Smedes, *Forgive and Forget. Healing the Hurts We Don't Deserve* (San Francisco: Harper & Row, Publishers, 1984) 152.

In response to a request from a friend, Dr. Thurman visited an old man who was very frail and ill. At their first meeting the elderly black gentleman declared, "You are looking at a man who cannot die." Before Dr. Thurman could comment, the man continued. "Not long before the war over slavery I barely escaped from the plantation with my life. I was accused of doing something I had not done. The master himself had me dragged to the empty smokehouse. I was stripped to the waist and my hands were tied to one of the cross beams. I was beaten until I fainted, then revived with buckets of cold water and flogged again. The next thing I remember was the darkness of the night and someone was cutting me loose and helping me to dress in fresh clothes that hurt my skin. Oh, Reverend, how it hurt! Whoever this was helped me to escape into the woods. Finally, I came to the river and got across the Ohio. Ever since I have been kept alive by hatred for the man who beat me. I suppose he has long since died . . . the only thing is I know I cannot die until I forgive him." Over the next several weeks Thurman dropped in to chat with the man occasionally. One morning as he entered the old gentleman's room, he was greeted with great excitement. All the man said was, "It happened last night! It happened." Immediately Thurman understood. In a few days the old man was dead.[4]

Forgiveness is a necessity whether the subject is living or dying. To be sure it is not easy. Quite honestly, I know far more about it theoretically than I can claim experientially. But God does not leave us alone with his expectation. He enables us to do what he requires us to do. With God's spirit we can be forgiving as well as forgiven.

Please heed the central word in this sermon. Every one of us needs to be a practitioner of forgiveness so what is past can be past, so we can know freedom in the present, so we can have hope for the future, and so we can pray honestly the prayer which our Lord taught us to pray: "Forgive us our trespasses as we forgive those who trespass against us." Amen.

---

[4]Howard Thurman, *With Head and Heart* (New York: Harcourt Brace Jovanovich, 1979) 71-72.

In the Beginning God

"In the beginning God. . . . " This statement of profundity and beauty is without parallel in literature generally and scripture specifically. Few, if any, declarations can match it in majesty and importance.

"In the beginning God. . . . " Please understand that this is not the observation of an eyewitness to creation but the confession of one who had come to know God in redemption. Historically the doctrine of creation developed relatively late in Israel's life. Only after the Israelites had learned of God's deliverance—at the Red Sea, in the wilderness, and at Meggido—did they come to assert God's sovereignty in creation. The confession "Yahweh the Creator" grew out of the declaration "Yahweh the Redeemer." People concluded that the one whom they had met in love had been there all along—indeed, from the very beginning.

The theological importance of Genesis 1:1 is beyond question. Here is an integral component in the biblical elaboration of faith. But of what, if any, value is the statement to us? Does it merely explain the beginning of things or is there more here—more of significance for the living of our days? I commend to you these four words as the substance of a statement with practical as well as theological significance. Take a look. It is

A Statement of Assurance

The world and its history began with a purposeful Creator—"In the beginning God." We are not mere products of some cosmic accident bumping around amid perpetual chaos. We are purpose-oriented persons—persons shaped in the image of the God who willed for us dignity, worth, fulfillment, and joy; the God who set creation in motion with a will for redemption. Trust, not tragedy, is the most fitting conclusion about it all.

But, what of disease, nonsense, and evil? These are not the products of a primal relentless fate. Rather, they are contradictions to the Creator's purpose. The God of beginnings is good. God intended good for the entirety of his creation. We can face life with courage rather than fear, with noble expectations rather than with grinding depression. The truth is not "In the beginning tragedy" but "In the beginning God." God is behind time and history and his purpose is sound, his ways are right.

The hymn writer Maltbie Babcock correctly perceived the assurance within the recognition of God as Creator. Babcock wrote:

This is my Father's world,
I rest me in the thought
Of rocks and trees, of skies and seas;
His hand the wonders wrought.

Genesis 1:1 is a statement of assurance and

A Statement of Priority

When you press life— really press it—for what is most important in it, ultimately you come to God. "In the beginning God." No person, object, or project is more basic than God. God is the beginning of everything and the source of meaning in relation to anything. Thus, our relationship with God is primary. If we are to be at one with the source of creation and redemption, the author of meaning, purpose, and joy, if we are to be attuned with the rhythm of life, we must be at one with God.

Notice carefully the order of priority. God precedes everything—even the Bible and the church. Our salvation comes only from God. So fundamentally important to life is God that, as Malcolm Muggeridge has observed, "If it were possible to live without God, it would not be worth living at all."[1]

"In the beginning God" is a statement of priority. It is also

A Statement of Security

When all else fails, God remains. When all else changes, God sustains. God, who is the ultimate priority, is the only source of real security.

Life does not always treat us kindly. Friends betray us. Lovers break their promises to us. Employers let us go. Groups leave us out. Aspirations

---

[1]Malcolm Muggeridge, *The End of Christendom* (Grand Rapids MI: William B. Eerdmans Publishing Company, 1980) 23.

turn into frustrations. Dreams are not realized. Exams are failed. However, at no point are we completely alone. At no time must we depend entirely upon our own resources. When life throws us, when the floor is jerked out from under us, God is there.

God prefers that we begin life together and live always in a harmonious relationship. However, God never fails to accept us wherever we are as we are. Thus, God gives us security even when we come to him hurting, guilty, frustrated, confused, and lonely.

I well remember a conversation with a young teenager dying with cancer. My pastor-friend sought to hear the boy out. He asked the terminally ill youth how he felt about God—was he angry with God, disappointed in God, or what. With wisdom far beyond his years, the young man explained, "God is all I have." Indeed, God is the ultimate security for all of us.

Genesis 1:1 is a statement of security. Also it is

A Statement of Responsibility

Simone Weil once said that "Creation was the moment that God ceased to be everything so that we humans could become something."[2] In other words, God set us on the stage of history and then demanded that we act. Responsibility is inherent in our identity.

Perhaps the word "stewardship" best describes our function in the world. Please recognize that it is not a matter of ownership. God created the world. All of life belongs to God. However, God set us in charge of the world. We have been made stewards of creation.

Our responsibility is to function according to the purposes of God's creativity. Thus, we seek to maintain unpolluted air, rich soil, clean streams and waterways, and the dignity of all persons. We honestly attempt to allow the earth to produce food enough for all people to eat. We sincerely labor to utilize the earth's resources so that every individual has adequate housing. We are stewards of creation. To fail to respect creation at any point or to harm creation in any manner is to sin against God. "In the beginning God."

---

[2]John Claypool, *Glad Reunion. Meeting Ourselves in the Lives of Bible Men and Women* (Waco TX: Word Books, 1985) 69.

We do not own the world but we are to serve as caretakers of it. What God created and declared to be "good," we are to maintain and share as good.

The opening verse of Genesis is a statement of responsibility. It is also

A Statement of Comfort

Understanding the impact of Genesis 1:1 well may lead to breathing a deep sigh of relief. Really to grasp the significance of "In the beginning God" is to find anxieties calmed, disappointments dispelled, and griefs comforted. Illnesses inflict us, problems beset us, difficulties confront us, deaths discourage us, and momentous challenges confront us. But, God is with us. "In the beginning God."

And, look at what we know about this God. Jesus said, "For God everything is possible" (Matthew 19:26). Do you grasp the meaning of that? "For God everything is possible!" We are not hemmed in. We are not down forever. We are not ultimately defeated. The presence of God is a source of comfort.

Paul plumbed the full significance of this awesome reality. Do not miss his words in Romans 8:

> If God is for us, who can be against us? . . . in all these things we have complete victory through him who loved us! For I am certain that nothing can separate us from his love: neither death nor life, neither angels nor other heavenly rulers or powers, neither the present nor the future, neither the world above nor the world below—there is nothing in all creation that will ever be able to separate us from the love of God which is ours through Christ Jesus our Lord.
> (Romans 8:31, 37-39 TEV)

What comfort! "In the beginning God" is a statement of comfort. Finally, allow me to suggest that it is also

A Statement of Hope

Implicit in all that has been said is the hope which Genesis 1:1 inspires. Creation is of God. Life is of God. Creation is so framed that within it we human beings are allowed to live and grow. Seasons come and go. We are drenched by both sunshine and rain. However, the forces around us are not hostile to us. God is in charge and God makes himself known to us as redeemer as well as creator.

The Deists missed this important truth. They surmised that God got creation going and then removed himself from the scene. Not so. God is the creator. But God has remained with his creation. God has been active in the history which he initiated. Most clearly he revealed himself in time and space in the person of Jesus Christ who fleshed out hope.

Listen to the witness of the writers of Scripture. The psalmist raised the question, "What, then, can I hope for, Lord?" and quickly answered, "I put my hope in you" (39:7). In the same spirit, the psalmist declared again, "Sovereign Lord, I put my hope in you" (71:5). Hear Jeremiah speak to God, "You are my place of safety (my hope!) when trouble comes" (17:17). The apostle Paul repeatedly expressed similar sentiments in different words.

To know "In the beginning God" is to take hope. This message is for you right now despite your frame of mind, your dominant emotions, the presence of problems. You can take hope. "In the beginning God."

Now, one thing more. "In the beginning God" is not just a statement related to the past. The truth involved has both a present and a future reference to it. The assurance, priority, security, responsibility, comfort, and hope of the statement are for today and tomorrow even as for yesterday. You can claim the promise of this sermon right now.

The writer of Revelation put the matter in its proper perspective. The divine voice declared, "I am the Alpha and the Omega, the first and the last, the beginning and the end" (22:13). My prayer is that what the scriptures assert consistently you will experience personally— "In the beginning God." In the end God. Now. Now God!

Christian Worship

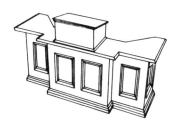

Wooden Worshipers

Deuteronomy 30:15-19; John 10:10

An interesting phenomenon from the romanticism of seventeenth- to nineteenth-century Europe, only recently discovered on my part, intrigues me. A popular feature of the courtly parks and grounds commonly filled with exotic animals was a hermit—an ornamental hermit actually. People felt that a holy-looking hermit made a pastoral scene even more inspirational. So much in demand was such a hermit that employers even ran advertisements seeking out individuals for the position. One such ad from a piece of eighteenth-century literature described Charles Hamilton's stipulations for the hermit job in Pains Hill Park, Surrey:

> The Hermit must remain in the Hermitage for at least seven years. He shall be provided with a Bible, optical Glasses, a Footmat, a Prayer Stool, an Hourglass, and with Water and Food from the House. He is to wear a Camelot Robe and must never, under any Circumstances, cut his Hair, his Beard, or his Nails, nor shall he leave the estate of Mr. Hamilton or speak with his Servants.[1]

Now here is the aspect of this whole story that most fascinates me. If no living hermit could be found to adorn the area, then a life-size hermit figure would do just as well. A 1793 writing described the Bayreuth Hermitage in Germany.

> Nine mossy Fathoms of Wood. . . . The Fathoms surrounded a Hermitage, which—because not a Soul at Court had the Makings of a live Hermit—was entrusted to a wooden one, who perched within, silently and sensibly, meditating and reflecting as much as is possible for such a Man. The Anchorite had been provided with a few ascetic Tomes, which fitted him properly, admonishing him to mortify his Flesh. . . .[2]

Comments were made about how ladies and gentlemen of the court strolled through these grounds and experienced shivers of inspiration run-

---

[1]Bernardin Schellenberger, *Nomad of the Spirit. Reflections of a Young Monastic,* trans. Joachim Neugraschel (New York: Crossroad, 1981) 13-14.
[2]Ibid., 14.

ning up and down their spines as they gazed at the solitary pious figure—
a mystical, hooded hermit made of wood—an ornamental hermit!

What a propensity people have to settle for show rather than substance. But, that is not a condition confined to ancient European romanticism. Such mentality is a fact of good old American reality. We delight
in great promises even if there is no fulfillment. Attractive paint adorns the
facade of an empty rotting building. Governments and businesses alike
employ banks of skilled public relations agents who can make a little look
like a lot, throw light on a mere trickle of meaningful activity in such a
manner that it looks like an enormous accomplishment. We want things to
look good even if things aren't good!

Now I must make a confession. When I first read this—funny if it were
not so true—account of ornamental hermits, my mind went to work play-
fully, if not deviously. Here is a way to solve the problem of empty seats
in any place of worship. If we just can recapture the ancient art form which
produced lifelike wooden monks, we can populate even the largest sanctuary if we wish, with wooden worshipers.

You laugh? Could we not use such images to fulfill some of the major
functions which many folks assign to a center for worship whether on the
campus of a university or in an area of a city? Think what impressive pictures we could get for our brochures. If the photographer did not shoot too
close in and catch some splintery protrusion from what should be a human
neck, the place would look pleasantly filled with worshipers. Never again
would we have to worry about whether or not a service would be well attended. Wooden worshipers never even leave the place of worship so they
do not have to remember to return. A consistently full chapel would be a
nice addition to this campus with very little effort once all the whittling
was completed. Passersby could glance in and be thrilled by the sight of a
crowded sanctuary, much like those early Europeans gloried in the vision
of an ascetic monk—whether a person or a plank. Ah, this would be a touch
of class.

What is wrong with that? Actually I can think of multiple benefits of
such a congregation. Everyone would be prompt. Services never would be
interrupted with coughing, whispering, or foot shuffling. No one would
disagree with the sermon. Controversy would be nonexistent.

Surely we can make a strong case for such an arrangement, given historical precedents in European romanticism and contemporary interests in
our culture. The show is the thing. Ironically we prefer even those corpses
which have been made to look most lifelike. We want the parade to pass

even if we never get to the circus. Though we may miss the messages and meanings of Christmas and Easter, we do not want to be deprived of the tinseled trees and lights, the lilies and the rabbits. We will settle for a lot less than what is real if it just can *seem* real.

Well I do hope that by now you are finding my hyperbolic ramblings to be ridiculous. In fact, I hope that you are almost ready to shout out "enough of that!" "Stop." Better still, I trust that you might be ready to resolve silently "that is not right" and to consider honestly the reasons why.

Why? What is wrong with this sermon up until now? However, we choose to express it, in our depths we know that the show is not enough. Symbol instead of substance cannot satisfy forever. Worship, real worship, must involve far more than ornamental participants. Worship centers need life. People should be present. Let me explain.

God Calls Us

True worship is a voluntary act of the willful adoration of God by persons created in the image of God and devoted to doing the will of God. That is God's desire. Thus, that is the nature of God's call to us, the divine summons for us. "Bless the Lord, O my soul . . . " (Psalm 103:1); "Make a joyful noise unto the Lord . . . " (Psalm 100:1); "O give thanks unto the Lord" (Psalm 106:1).

Of course, the all-powerful ruler of the universe can assure worship, mandate an exaltation of his nature by means of manipulation. But that would be little better than a Charlie McCarthy act on the part of deity—a ventriloquist-like throwing of the divine voice through wooden-mouthed dummies; a kind of cosmic marionette show with the Sovereign of the world meticulously pulling the strings of puppets and making them say all that he wants to hear. But, that is not worship. How can words and acts be authentically worshipful if they stem from persons incapable of any other words and acts?

God calls forth from us the very kind of behavior which pleases him and nurtures us. The first line of the old catechetical statement is right on target—the chief end of a person is to glorify God and to enjoy him forever. Ernest Campbell reflected on this basic teaching. "Why not such adoration?" he asked, "Why are we who know so well the gospel story so unable to be moved by his presence and his power? After all, he has kindled fires of affection, induced more liberality, elicited more faith in God, encouraged and effected more reconciliation, inspired more art, set in motion more song and poetry than any other man that ever lived"[3] Indeed, why not such adoration?

Truthful, personal participation is essential. God wants no part of performance without purpose. Even a quick reading of the prophets will dispel any thoughts about divine pleasure over a show without substance, festivals without faith. Through his servant Amos, God spoke to Israel, "I hate your religious festivals; I cannot stand them!" (Amos 5:21).

God calls unto himself a people, a people for worship, not a collection of robot-natured look-alikes who boringly beep out praise; not an assembly of ornamental Christians ever so proper but ever so stiff-necked and hard-hearted. Stammering, stuttering pilgrims; frustrated, frightened believers; awkward, inexperienced disciples; ashamed, burdened sinners— yes, God exults in the true worship of these kinds of people, a sincerely offered worship which is much preferred to the carefully orchestrated gimmickry of a good show.

God calls persons—persons like us. Then, too . . .

We Need Each Other

In some moments I almost succumb to a rather tragic point of view which finds expression in *The Wizard of Oz*. Remember, the Tin Man wanted a heart. He was told that he did not know how lucky he was not to have a heart. The rationale was that hearts will never be practical until they can be made unbreakable. Who of us has not hurt so badly as to understand such thought? Yet, think of the dynamics in a community of people with hearts—people with the capacity to laugh and to cry, to mourn and to celebrate, to understand and to care. We need relationships with persons whose hearts have been broken, for from such come forgiveness, healing, salvation.

I have told the story many times, but repeatedly it speaks to me profoundly. One day over lunch Carlyle Marney recalled a conversation with his seventy-five-year-old father. His father said, "I wish I could go back to the first day I became a Christian and start all over. My faith would be firm." Much surprised, Marney said, "Daddy, I would have bet my life

---

[3]Ernest T. Campbell, *Locked in a Room with Open Doors* (Waco, Texas: Word Books, 1974) 70.

it had always been firm.'' ''No,'' the father replied, ''it's been shot full of doubts.'' Then Marney asked his dad how he had kept going, what had caused him to hold on to the faith. The old man said, ''My faith would be alright if I could get to the meeting.''

Yes! Yes. If we can just get to the meeting. We need each other. But additionally . . .

The World Waits For Us

Rightly understood and properly expressed, the worship of God results in service to his creation and to his creatures. We cannot stay in a sanctuary all the time. We should not. And, no reason exists to replace us with mannequins so the house of worship always looks full. Sometimes the house of worship needs to be empty! Worshipers are needed elsewhere—in a classroom, in a hospital ward, in the streets, beside a person who is hurting, with a group planning social strategy, before a city council deliberating welfare policies.

Within worship we find the strength for faithfulness, the courage to express as well as to hold convictions. Meditations on the Bread of Life motivate persons to take all kinds of bread to hungry people. Studies of Jesus calming a storm or silencing a demoniac send us out to soothe the tumultuous forces which rack our friends and communities. Regular attendance in the house of God causes attentiveness to the housing conditions of the people around us. Worship of God's nature awakens us to his passion for justice, for peace, for liberty, for mercy, for grace, and enlists us in those causes.

The world waits for us, mostly without knowing it. Yet, in worship we are at the source of help for most all hurt. To us—to worshipers—is given the awesome privilege of translating belief into behavior, faith into faithfulness, moral convictions about righteousness into social actions which are right.

Wooden worshipers, ornamental Christians cannot do it. But that is not who we are. We are not here for the show. The purpose of this meeting is not to add to our campus a lovely touch of class. We are here to worship God and to make a difference for good in our world. Let no one ever confuse sincere worshipers with ornamentation!

What is the purpose of all of this? What is the message to be wrung from this somewhat strange sermon? I offer to you an affirmation concerning the centrality of personal involvement in worship growing out of our corporate life. I strongly encourage you toward that end. And, of course, at the same time, I plead with you not ever to settle merely for the show of faith but to grapple persistently with its substance.

Now, let us praise God, not routinely as some purchased decoration, but as a lively, purposeful congregation of God's people!

Problems with Prayer

Psalm 5:1-3; Matthew 6:5-13; Romans 8:26-27

A major peril of the pastoral ministry is that of becoming convinced of the need for a particular sermon and personally knowing precious little about the subject involved and the biblical texts to be treated. Temptations abound: to shrink any issue to a size that is manageable; to render every truth practical; to eliminate all complexity so that everything is understandable; to convey the impression that I am an expert on the subjects which I address, that I preach as an accomplished professional. More often than not, Christian proclamation mandates an engagement with mystery— divine mystery. Thus, frequently I find myself uncomfortable— prompted to treat biblical passages which I cannot explain, to affirm truths with which I still grapple, to commend behavior which I have not mastered; indeed, to preach as much to myself as to other people.

In the preparation of this sermon, those temptations and that realization were set before me with exceptional strength. A confession of inadequacy is the only valid point of departure in the introduction to what follows. My concern is with prayer.

To be sure, I believe in prayer, appreciate the power of prayer, and seek to pray. I must tell you, though, that what I do not know about prayer far exceeds what I know and that for me praying is not an easy discipline. Not surprisingly, I have some difficulty (maybe it is envy) with those persons who can drop a prayer like dropping a hat, explain the dynamics of prayer like diagraming the intricacies of a machine, and claim a long line of exact answers as if they had God on a string.

Sometime back, I set down for my own benefit some of the uses of prayer which are most prevalent from my observations. I sought to make the list apart from any exercise of judgment regarding the rightness or wrongness of items on it. I failed. Here is a part of my review.

Prayer as Instruction

Some prayers ostensibly offered to God are made, in reality, media for announcements to a group of people. That which is overlooked or omitted elsewhere is incorporated by a prayer. ''Father, you know that tonight's meeting begins at 6:30 and that it is so important that all of our members be present for it. We ask you to be with us and we thank you for enabling us to provide child care for those who need it." At times the subject matter is not so mundane. "O Lord, we pray your blessings on the Jones family who last week experienced a fire in their house and now need your help. Bless those who are willing to bring items of clothing and cans of food to the fellowship hall for this cause." "Father, we remember to you the chief executive of our local industry. He needs to be saved."

To whom are we speaking? What is our purpose in such praying? In addition to commenting about others, some people seem to pray in order to convey information about themselves. "God, I just love you more than other people do." "Lord, you know that I have offered to sacrifice everything for you."

Does God need to be informed by us? Does the All-Knowing Sovereign of the Universe require instructions regarding the logistics of our meetings or reminders about the specifics of our commitments? Is God eager for our explanations?

Many years ago at one of our Southern Baptist theological seminaries, students regularly ate all of their meals together. Responsibility for offering the blessing prior to each meal was assigned. Predictably, this time of prayer had become an occasion for a demonstration of academic acumen. One student, strongly impressed with his own learning, incorporated a Greek phrase in his prayer of thanksgiving and followed it with the explanation "which being interpreted, God, means. . . . " I am sure that God was relieved to have the matter explained.

Prayer as information. Then, there is . . .

Prayer as Evasion

Prayer is often appropriated as an apparently pious way of sidestepping pertinent issues. Problems which cry out for resolution are addressed with admonitions to pray faithfully rather than with encouragement to act helpfully. Critical needs of the university are discussed, difficulties in interpersonal relationships are examined, and frightening social challenges are confronted. Someone raises the question, "What are we going to do?" Almost invariably, a voice intones, "Let's pray about it."

Please do not misunderstand. In no sense do I wish to discourage the practice of prayer in relation to any issue, about all concerns. However, I do want to call into question the tendency to use prayer as a means of evasion. Biblically, prayer and Christian action are two sides of one coin. That about which we pray is that on which we need to act. And, that on which we act is that about which we need to pray.

Matters of conscience such as hunger, war, prejudice, jealousy, and the like appropriately belong in our prayers. However, to resolve to pray about these matters is not enough in itself. Statements of such an intention can serve as subtle forms of evasion. Prayers about hunger must be complemented by actions which make available food, prayers about war by efforts aimed at making peace, prayers about prejudice by work on love, and prayers about jealousy by nurturing patience and understanding.

Prayer as evasion. In reality, the two cannot endure together. By its very nature, prayer requires engagement. Another use of prayer involves . . .

Prayer as Sanction

I do not mind being asked to voice prayers of invocation and benediction at various events. Honestly, though, I have delivered prayers in some situations which I left with confusion as to why prayer even had been requested. My fear is that prayer is used occasionally, maybe frequently, in order to associate a particular event, person, or institution with Almighty God. Prayer is a kind of tip of the hat to God in order to associate God with our plans—whether or not God wants to be associated—to imply divine affirmation for our self-styled actions.

Why do we pray before a political rally—in order to lobby with God on the part of a particular candidate or to imply a divine blessing for a particular party? Why do we pray before a football game—could God possibly care who wins?

Too many times I have been in gatherings which invoked the divine name at their beginnings before quickly forgetting any divine relation and rushing on through their self-willed intentions to arrive at their predetermined conclusions. I well remember a committee meeting in which the "amen" of the opening prayer was followed immediately by the comment, "We can do all of the research which you desire on this matter but my mind is made up and I am ready to vote."

Prayer is inappropriate as an attempt to give divine sanction to that which really has no divine relation. If it is our idea or plan we should stand by it and not seek to salvage some divine accountability for it by means of a prayer. Prayer as sanction. One other use of prayer embraces . . .

Prayer as Manipulation

At stake may be a purpose so simple as that of quieting an audience in order to start a meeting. Amid the clamor of numerous conversations, a presiding officer says, "Let us pray." Other motives are more problematic. A church committee session is split by conflicting opinions. Suddenly a leader suggests the need for prayer. Argumentative voices are silenced, heads are bowed, and the following words are offered, "Help us, O God, that as we pray we will be able to see things the same way. Enable those who are opposed to our plan to see the rightness of the endeavor and the weakness of their opinions." A parent can manipulate a child in such a pious-sounding manner— "Help Johnny to see the evil of his present ways and to understand that my desire for him is not just the wish of his mother but your will, O Lord." Prayer as manipulation.

Well, enough of that. You realize, of course, that what I have been describing are not prayers at all. A horse is not a cow simply because it is called a cow. Instructions, evasions, sanctions, and manipulation are not prayer merely because they are labeled prayer.

Actually, even to speak of the uses of prayer is an inappropriate means of missing a crucial point, like raising the question, "Does prayer really work?" Such talk is indicative of functional considerations which suggest that prayer is a kind of spiritual gimmick. "Say the right words and you will get good results." To speak of "using" prayer is to misunderstand the very nature of prayer. What is involved?

Prayer is essentially a posture of radical openness to God. Emphasis here must fall on the terms "radical openness." Praying is akin to standing before God with arms outstretched and hands open; vulnerable to God in every aspect of our being. Even to begin to pray is to acknowledge that we are not God and to admit that we want to be in touch with God. An investigation of God's will, a discovery of the divine desire, constitute our uppermost aim. Thus, waiting, listening, reaching out, and searching are even more important than speaking.

Did you catch the thrust of Paul's comment in the Romans passage? "The Spirit . . . comes to help us. . . . For we do not know how we ought to pray" (8:26 TEV). At its best praying is provoked by the presence of God's Spirit in us, not prompted by our planned petitions. In genuine prayer, we may not have the right words on the tips of our tongues or in the recesses of our souls. At times we may be at a loss even to know how to proceed. Then in vulnerable openness, we allow God's Spirit to say through us what needs to be said.

If you think praying is easy, surely you must have in mind some other activity. Radical openness and extreme vulnerability are never exacted except at great price. We are persons who like to protect our privacy, hedge our bets, play things close to our chests. Little wonder that many of us can be caused to skip our prayers completely or to be distracted from our prayers easily. Praying is as difficult and draining as it is critical.

Within a posture of radical openness before God, one other dimension of prayer about which I am certain becomes clear.

Prayer is basically a process of personal communication with God. As general as it is, I must leave it at that. I can no more tell you how you should pray than I can instruct you on how to talk with your parents, your spouse, or your best friend. The words must be your words, the style your style. Both must be totally honest, nonpretentious, wholly authentic. Properly understood, prayer is the most profound opportunity for honesty that any individual ever experiences. In prayer, honesty never carries a penalty. Just the opposite. Only when there is complete honesty can prayer be a possibility.

Personally, I take great comfort in Paul's promise of the assistance of God's Spirit. Many times I do not know how to begin a prayer or how to proceed in prayer—maybe my joy is too great or my grief too heavy, my praise too awkward or my doubts too prevalent. Often I would like to escape prayer altogether. I do not want to communicate with God. I like my ideas. I desire no challenge to my thoughts. I am comfortable with my plans. Thus, for me, praying frequently means unloading painfully. I have to work at it and squirm with it. Words come only as concerns are ripped from my conscience and thoughts torn from my soul.

Henri Nouwen was exactly right when he observed that if people feel a little praying cannot do any harm, they will discover it cannot do much good either.[1] No such thing exists as offering a little prayer here and there. Prayer involves the totality of one's being. Praying is costly. But, like breathing, it is necessary to real living.

Radical openness before God and honest communication with God—for me, these are the essential ingredients in prayer. As so often is the case,

---

[1]Henri J. M. Nouwen, *With Open Hands* (Notre Dame IN: Ave Maria Press, 1978) 94.

thankfully God helps us to do what he asks us to do. Thus, our tendency toward conditions, limits, and brackets and our propensity for calculated thoughts and measured words are transformed by God's Spirit who works in us and prays through us. The goal is communion—life with God and in God, God's life in us.

A prayer found on the bombed-out ruins of Coventry Cathedral is worthy of our appropriation. Contained in its words is a concept of the true nature of prayer, an understanding which moves us from speaking about the problems of prayer to recognizing the promises of prayer.

Hallowed be Thy Name

In Industry	God be in my hands and in my making.
In the Arts	God be in my senses and in my creating.
In the Home	God be in my heart and in my loving.
In Commerce	God be at my desk and in my trading.
In Suffering	God be in my pain and in my enduring.
In Government	God be in my plans and in my deciding.
In Education	God be in my mind and in my growing.
In Recreation	God be in my limbs and in my leisure.

Holy, Holy, Holy Lord God of Hosts
Heaven and Earth are full of thy glory!

Amen and Amen.

Toward a Recovery of Wonder

Mark 2:1-12

Those of us in the free-church tradition have labored at making faith a part of the ebb and flow of common experience. In our pragmatic minds, the imminence of Christ and the relevance of belief are considered primary. Transcendence has been treated almost as a problem. Nowhere is the earthly oriented nature of our bias more apparent than in the forms of our worship places and practices. Rigidly we have resisted symbols and rituals. Deliberately we have stressed informality, folksiness, and commonality.

Almost completely absent from such thought and practice is the idea of mystery. Yet, our God is Holy Other and Wholly Other. His ways are not our ways. His thoughts are not our thoughts. More than one theologian has pointed out that without the element of mystery there is no religion and no real faith.

What has happened to our sense of wonder? In recent days I have come to believe that issue—the absence of wonder—is critical. Apart from wonder, we will not know a life that is really bountiful or a worship that is truly spiritual. Even our evangelism and missions will suffer, because no one is won to Christ by argument. Faith is a response to mystery. As many people have noted, true religion is caught, not taught.

Study the human experience of God as recorded in Scripture. Key words are amazement and wonder. Actual actions document this observation. See Moses taking off his sandals to stand on holy ground. Read of Ezekiel bowing before the mystery in the sky. Hear Isaiah detail his encounter with the holy presence in the temple. Look at Paul blinded by the divine light on the Damascus road.

Counsel to live with wonder is implicit throughout the Bible. According to one extrabiblical source, Jesus made the counsel explicit. In a brief quotation attributed to Matthias, the man elected to replace Judas among the Twelve, and preserved in a work by Clement of Alexandria, Jesus purportedly is quoted as saying, ''Wonder at the things before you, for wonder is the way to knowledge."[1] The authenticity of this statement from Jesus is supported dramatically by words on one of the Oxyrhynchus papyri found just south of Cairo, Egypt. On this document is the written assertion, "Jesus, on whom be peace, hath said, 'Wonder at the things before you, laying this down as the first step toward the knowledge that lies beyond.'"[2] Wonder is the way to knowledge!

Reasons for wonder are all around us. Chesterton was correct, "The world does not lack for wonders, only for a sense of wonder."[3]

Could that have been one of the attributes Jesus was commending when he admonished us to become as little children? A child relishes an experience first and only later seeks to explain it. Children are not afraid to express themselves fully, to give themselves completely to moments of meaning and joy.

Why can we not come to the gospel with the wonder and anticipation of a child approaching Christmas morning? Where is the place of awe in our religious experience? One writer has told how some Indian people can hardly receive the truth of Christianity because to them it seems too good to be true. Can you identify with that?

Of course, I think I know the source of the problem—familiarity, deadening familiarity. One day in a little Swiss village high in the Alps, I stood awestruck staring at those snowcapped peaks flanked by brilliant green meadows. All around me people tended to their business as usual. My vista was their backyard. They were familiar with all of that which to me was spectacular. Similarly, in the Louvre in Paris, I stood gazing in amazement at a famous work of art. My attention was captivated and my spirit soared. Around me a guard and a housekeeper went about their chores with not even so much as a glance at the object of my wonderment. In Eastern Europe, I watched Romanians arrive for worship services two or three hours in advance and then give themselves completely to singing, praying, and preaching for another two to three hours. What was just another service for me was a cause of special wonder to those for whom religious liberty is not a reality.

---

[1]Leslie Weatherhead, *Steady in an Unsteady World,* ed. Stephen A. Odom (Valley Forge PA: Judson Press, 1986) 51.

[2]Ibid., 53.

[3]William Sloane Coffin, *Living the Truth in a World of Illusions* (San Francisco: Harper & Row, Publishers, 1985) 42.

Deadening familiarity. Wonder is blunted almost completely. We have heard it all before, this business of Christian truth. Who has not had ample opportunities to attend regular worship services, to sing well-known hymns, to read often-read gospel texts, and to listen to traditional biblical expositions? Even talk of conversion—Christian conversion—is somewhat cheap. Everyone needs to make a profession of faith in Christ and unite with a church. Usually this can be done by age twelve. Most all people know that and most all people do that in one way or another. Gone is wonder.

Not much captivates our attention anymore in any realm. Transcendence seems irretrievably lost. We may sing "this is my Father's world" but we approach it as just so much mastered science. One evening an elderly gentleman took a young child out to look at and to enjoy a brilliant starry sky. The lad's one comment was a question, "Which ones did we put up there?"

Where now is a sense of transcendence? Do we have any perception of mystery? If wonder is indeed the way to knowledge, what does that say about what we know, how we educate, and what we do?

Once a great sea painter was searching for a boy in whose face he might find the wonder of the sea. He chose not a lad from the seacoast to whom the seacoast was nothing special, but a boy from the London slums—a child who had never seen the ocean![4]

Maybe that is the clue we need. Can you recall how you felt the first time, *the first time,* you saw the ocean, you smelled a rose, you found a four-leaf clover, or you witnessed a snowfall? What if you had never seen a sunset until now? More to the point here, can you remember your conversion to Christ and the manner in which you approached your baptism? Can you identify at all with the woman who confessed, "It is wonderful—wonder full!—to be a Christian?"

Well, what difference does it make anyway? Why is wonder that significant? Believe me, it makes a tremendous difference in every place of worship. Let wonder be recovered and watch out. Regularly worship centers will be filled to overflowing. But, let wonder be lost and worship will not be that important—only a take-it-or-leave-it, a come-and-go affair.

---

[4]Ernest T. Campbell, *Locked in a Room with Open Doors* (Waco TX: Word Books, Publisher, 1974) 69.

However, more is at stake than attendance and participation in corporate worship.

One's whole view of life is affected by the presence or the absence of wonder. With wonder come the possibility of surprise and the availability of hope. People who have retained a sense of wonder know that existence is not predictable. Surprise occurs—sometimes surprises of great joy. Life can change—for the better, so much for the better. Hope— that element so much needed and so much in short supply right now—hope pulsates in the innermost recesses of a wondering heart.

I wish I had words to do what is needed. I ache for the ability to offer a description of wonder which will aid the recovery of wonder. Think about it. Really think about it. Better still, feel it as you ponder it. Ours is the joy of being loved by the God of creation. The divine being who watches over every sparrow cares infinitely for you and me. God loves us! We do not have to bear needless guilt. Regardless of what we have done and of whom we have wronged, we can know forgiveness. Forgiveness! Our sins are treated by God as if we never committed them. To us has been given the opportunity to know eternal life—a quality of life so good that it is indescribable apart from God. We are invited to join with all of creation in the praise and adoration of God. Our words, our prayers, and our songs can make a difference in the exaltation of the divine name.

What is common about such a life? And, this is only the beginning. We live in a world in which the spirit of the resurrected Christ is free to transform moments and events as well as people. To us has been given the capacity to love—really to love—to know joy, to experience peace—the peace that passes all understanding. We are freed from decision making by cold calculations and for relations making which defies rational explanations. Our faith is more poetry than science. We are ever alive to the rhythms of creation and to those events which only can be described as miracles— facilitators of a new creation.

How do you see it? Remember the words attributed to Jesus: "Wonder at the things before you, for wonder is the way to knowledge." I pray that you will come alive to that which is in you, around you, and beyond you.

For years I have profited from Elizabeth Barrett Browning's poetry:

Earth's crammed with heaven,
And every common bush afire with God;
But only he who sees takes off his shoes,
The rest sit round it and pluck blackberries.[5]

Do you see? Do you wonder?

It is high time for us to get our shoes off! Let us move together to that position envisioned in the hymn writer's conclusion—"lost in wonder—lost in wonder—love, and praise."[6] Amen.

---

[5]Elizabeth Barrett Browning, *The Complete Poetical Works of Elizabeth B. Browning* (Saint Clair Shores MI: Scholarly Press, Inc., 1972).

[6]Charles Wesley, "Love Divine, All Loves Excelling," 1743.

Loving God

Permit me a very personal question. Do you love God? Before you answer too hastily or react defensively, allow me to make a plea for complete honesty. Think seriously about it. Do you really love God?

Quite frankly, I am raising the question with you because of my own incessant interaction with this interrogation recently. For the past several weeks, I have thought long and hard about this matter of loving God. What is the essence of my relationship with God? Do I really love God?

For the moment, I am making a distinction between loving God and worshiping God or obeying God. I have sought to worship God and to obey God for most of my life. In fact, a preoccupation with worship and obedience stands behind my examination of love. Rabbi Harold Kushner set me to thinking when he wrote that obedience is not the highest of religious virtues.[1] Suddenly I realized that for years I may have had the cart before the horse. At their best, worship and obedience are expressions of love, not substitutes for love or preludes to love. What God desires most is not my worship or my obedience but my love, real love.

Actually much of my religious life may have been devoted to efforts aimed at earning or justifying God's love for me. Surely if I am obedient to God's law I can be the recipient of God's love. If God is the beneficiary of my adoration, certainly he will shower me with his compassion. You know the rationalizations. In such a religious posture, it is possible for God to have our obedience and worship but not our love. Do you really love God?

Whether or not we love God depends to a great extent on how we view God. How do you see God? Philosophy has done a bad number on us—formally or informally. God is imaged as a giant abstraction, an ill-defined transcendent entity. We talk of God as primal truth, the unmoved mover,

---

[1]Harold S. Kushner, *When All You've Ever Wanted Isn't Enough. The Search for a Life That Matters* (New York: Summit Books, 1986) 127.

the ground of our being, the first cause, the *summum bonum*. Such language is so impersonal. How does one love an "unmoved mover"? More distinctly religious terminology has not fared much better. God is creator of the universe or author of redemption. Abstraction remains.

Ethicists have made a contribution to our dilemma. God has been depicted as the great lawgiver or rules maker. At an extreme, religion has been reduced to a matter of bookkeeping—the maintenance of a spiritual report card related to what has been done and what has been left undone.

How do you see God? As a fearful tyrant? A nagging parent? An authoritative teacher? A dictatorial ruler? How you see God will determine whether or not you love God. I believe that some of my earliest conceptions of God evoked fear and encouraged obedience but omitted love. That well may be a characterization of all religious immaturity.

Jesus helped us immensely when he revealed God as Father. God is personal and capable of intimacy. Nouwen may be right in his observation that the best definition of revelation is the uncovering of the truth that it is safe to love. Conversion is a discovery of the possibility of living by love. How do you see God?

Whether or not we love God depends also upon how we view religion, how we understand the divine-human relationship. What stands at the heart of religion? Most people will answer goodness. Typically interpreted, being religious is equated with being good. An awe that borders on fear causes persons to concentrate on divine commandments. Punishment is bandied about as the consequence of disobedience. Thus, keeping the rules is the way to play it safe, to live properly.

Readily you see that from this perspective religion is a burden to be carried rather than a faith by which we are liberated. Persons can obey God meticulously and attend worship services regularly, yet miss out on loving God completely.

Maybe the most fundamental question to be raised is not how we view God or how we understand religion but how God views us. What is God's will?

Study the Scriptures. Repeatedly you encounter conformity without compassion. Numerous persons obeyed God's laws but failed to return God's love. The legalists were not lovers. They seldom are. Prime proponents of this point of view were the Pharisees. Here were persons long on moral purity but short on genuine compassion. They cared more for rules than for people. Ironically, sadly, they could revel in the revelation of law but kill the incarnation of love. God desires more than obedience.

Likewise, worship is not sufficient to satisfy God's will. Read the prophets. God actually came to hate the religious festivals, the worship rituals, of the people of Israel. They were devoid of love.

God does not desire legalistic marionettes or immature devotees of ritual. Seek out the dominant biblical imagery and repeatedly you will stumble upon love. Love! Love—that is what God desires, love between God and mature individuals who have the affectionate sensitivities of a child. What are the pervasive biblical pictures of the divine-human relationship? Lover and beloved. Bride and bridegroom. Robert Capon is correct, "The glory and the misery of the love affair is the master image for the understanding of our vocation."[2] My responsibility to God is that of a lover to the beloved. The essence of Christianity is a relationship—a covenant relationship between two passionate lovers.

Most essential in this covenant relationship is not our perfection morally or our worship ritually but our love personally. God desires a love affair with people of integrity—people who are all they are meant to be. "The will of God is . . . his longing that we will take the risk of being nothing but ourselves, desperately in love"[3]—in love with God.

I read the devotional classics of our faith and I discover again and again the centrality of a love for God. Francis of Assisi was described as a lover of God—one whose love for God was as passionate and ecstatic as that of a troubadour's love for his lady. Something is very right about that.

I want the essence of my faith to be trust in a loving relationship. I realize now that I do not have to earn God's love. That is a given. I want love to dominate my relationship to God.

I want to pray not because I am supposed to pray or because I am hard-pressed by certain problems but because I want to commune with my lover. I desire to share everything openly—the bad and the good—and to make known my ultimate concerns honestly. I want to sing not because some order of worship indicates that it is time to sing but because music is the mood of my heart. I am in love and that love seeks expression through a whistle, a shout, or a song. No longer do I view sin as a breaking of the rules. Now I see it as the violation of a relationship. I do not want to sin

---

[2]Robert Farrar Capon, *Hunting the Divine Fox. An Introduction to the Language of Theology* (New York: The Seabury Press, 1985) 41.
[3]Ibid.

because I do not want to hurt my beloved, to cause grief in God. I want to love God. Do you love God?

Well, what is love for God? According to the biblical analogies we can get some glimpses of what ought to take place between persons and God by looking at love affairs between individuals. I do not know the best means of interpretation for the biblical book we know as The Song of Songs, but I do believe that in the personal, sensitive, selective, and exclusive love found there we can discover something of a model for our love for God. Ponder some of the phrases:

O thou whom my soul loveth (1:7),

Have you seen him whom my soul loves? (3:3)

Obviously, a lover is addressing his beloved. Unquestionably, it is a model for our relationship with God.

What is love for God? Perhaps we best inquire, "What is love?" Years ago Richard Niebuhr sought to answer this profound question. Little can be done to improve upon his elaboration. Niebuhr wrote, "Love is rejoicing over the existence of the beloved one, it is the desire that he be rather than not be . . . it is happiness in the thought of him; it is profound satisfaction over everything that makes him great and glorious."[4] Is not our love for God an exultation in the very existence of God, elation over God's nature, happiness over the fact that God is? Hear Niebuhr again, "Love is gratitude: it is thankfulness for the existence of the beloved; it is the happy acceptance of everything that he gives without the jealous feeling that the self ought to be able to do as much; it is gratitude that does not seek equality; it is wonder over the other's gift of himself in companionship."[5] Do these words not get at our response to God's creation? Certainly they encapsulate our reaction to divine grace and redemption. Niebuhr again: "Love is reverence: it keeps its distance even as it draws near; it does not seek to absorb the other in the self or want to be absorbed by it; it rejoices in the otherness of the other; it desires the beloved to be what he is and does not seek to refashion him into a replica of the self or to make him a means to the self's advancement. As reverence, love is and seeks knowledge of the other, not by way of curiosity nor for the sake of gaining power but in

---

[4]H. Richard Niebuhr, *The Purpose of the Church and Its Ministry* (New York: Harper & Row, 1956) 35, cited in Richard John Neuhaus, *Freedom for Ministry* (San Francisco: Harper & Row, Publishers, 1979) 83.

[5]Ibid.

rejoicing and in wonder.''[6] Is this not the desire of true devotion? Consider Niebuhr one more time, ''Love is loyalty: it is the willingness to let the self be destroyed rather than that the other cease to be; it is the commitment of the self by self-binding will to make the other great. It is loyalty, too, to the other's cause—to his loyalty.''[7]

Did you hear that conclusion? Now we can speak of worship and obedience. Worship and obedience are acts of love. God's cause is our cause. His ways are our ways.

Carlyle Marney liked to point out that love can only be said with verbs and every verb is a verb of relation. As usual, Marney was right. The essence of real love is giving—giving to the beloved.

In addition to exulting in the being of God, genuinely liking his divine nature, real love for God involves also taking up God's cause as one's own. Thus love is more than mere emotion, tenderness, and tears; it is involvement in justice, commitment to ministry, and engagement in peace.

We serve God not because we have fear before him, not because of the imposition of rules from him, but because of our love for him. The work of justice is a labor of joy. Peacemaking is a real blessing. Reconciliation is an act of devotion. Worship is the natural outgrowth of adoration. We love God. So, we serve God. Our service defines our love.

If we love God, we love what and whom God loves. That is why John could write that if we say we love God and hate our neighbor, we lie. Loving God and loving other persons are complementary actions. The latter grows out of the former.

What is love for God? What is love? It is rejoicing in the presence of the beloved. It is gratitude. It is reverence and loyalty. It is service. Love for God is all of that and more. It is worship and obedience.

To be a Christian is to be head over heels in love with God—it is that simple; to love God with all of one's heart, soul, mind, and strength—it is that costly. At present, my most basic desire is to love God. How about you? I commend such love to you. To love God—genuinely to love God—is our greatest duty and our highest joy.

---

[6]Ibid., 84.
[7]Ibid.

Listening—A Spiritual Discipline

Psalm 66:16-19; Romans 10:14-17

If you were asked to name the most essential spiritual disciplines, how would you respond? Chances are that you would speak about prayer, meditation, Bible study, worship, and various forms of ministry. Most likely, few people, if any, would include listening on their list. Yet, from a biblical perspective and in actual experience listening is a profoundly important spiritual discipline that needs constant nurturing.

Repeatedly God has addressed his people with the imperative "Listen!" Consider the preface to the most basic text in all of Judaism—"Hear, O Israel" (Deuteronomy 6:4)—in the Old Testament and a directive integral to the teaching of Jesus—"Hear and understand" (Matthew 15:10)—in the New Testament. Through the years, prophets and apostles, priests and preachers, have relayed the divine counsel regarding listening. According to Paul, people do not come to redemptive faith without hearing (Romans 10:14, 17). According to James, persons with a mature faith are "quick to hear" and "slow to speak" (James 1:19). Apart from strict adherence to this recurrent biblical admonition to listen, holy commandments and divine promises go unheeded and life is fragmented.

Who can dispute the priority of listening? Shakespeare dubbed not listening a disturbing disease. Oliver Wendell Holmes labeled listening the privilege of wisdom. But, quite honestly, listening is as much a difficulty as it is a necessity, a spiritual priority. We have a propensity to speak. Usually our first reaction to almost any situation is "What can I say?" or "What should I say?" We view as highly unusual those occasions on which we are speechless. So much time and attention are devoted to talking that little consideration is left for listening.

Of course, almost anyone can understand our preoccupation with speaking and near aversion to listening. When we are talking we are in charge, somewhat in control of things; we are calling the shots. When we are listening, we are vulnerable. The one speaking can direct our attention, affect our emotions, and call us to action. When we listen carefully we run the risk of confronting new ideas, considering unwelcome subjects, and coping with criticisms. Frankly, it is much safer as well as easier to speak than to listen.

No one ever promised that any spiritual discipline would be easy, only that all are essential. Listening is no exception. Consider the importance of listening as a spiritual discipline.

Listening is an avenue to knowing oneself.

Earl Koile has written: "Our sense of identity and part of our nature as human beings hinge on our ways of talking and listening to ourselves. We distinguish ourselves from one another and from other parts of nature through our ways of feeling and sharing who we are."[1] In much the same vein, Wendell Johnson has observed, "A man is never so serene as when he hears himself out. . . . Nor is he ever so gravely ill as when he stops his tongue. . . . By stopping up our own ears against the sound of our own voices, we achieve not the peace of inner stillness, but the unnerving disquietude of haunted consciousness."[2]

What most influences your words and actions—the endless sales pitches which bombastically fill the airwaves, the expectations expressed by friends, the call sounded by the crowd, the norms named by our culture? What do you say? What do you hear from deep inside your own being? Each of us needs to listen to that. If we do not listen to ourselves, we will never know ourselves.

It is not through always expressing ourselves to others but through regularly listening to the expressions of others that we increase our own self-awareness. Listening to others puts us in touch with reality and causes us to grapple with what is of value. As I hear the sounds around me I discover that which I cherish within me. Listening to other persons is a means of exploring my own person. Even self-esteem and feelings of self-worth are wrapped up in our listening.

Perceptive psychologists have pointed out that the conditions for becoming—that is, finding oneself and developing personal potentials to the

---

[1]Earl Koile, *Listening as a Way of Becoming* (Waco TX: Regency Books, 1977) 21-22.
[2]Ibid., 127.

fullest extent—are the same as those for listening. In listening we come to know our own individuality and to experience liberty.

Listening is a means of ministering to others.

Rarely a week goes by that I do not hear the sentiment expressed, "I just need someone to listen to me." "All I want is to be heard." Usually a person with that confession will be heard one way or another.

When an individual feels unheard, that individual may become frustrated, angry, even hostile. The person may well set in motion forces which result in severe alienation. All kinds of erratic, irresponsible, volatile behavior develop among people who feel that they have no one to listen to them.

Just think how many chasms between human relationships, gaps between various groups, could be bridged by careful listening. In so many instances, people are angry with each other because they feel unheard. Misunderstandings between racial groups, conflicts between faculties and administrators, arguments between husbands and wives, confusion between parents and children could be resolved by the simple practice of the spiritual discipline of listening.

To listen to another person is to show compassion for that person, to take that individual seriously, to open up the possibility of a meaningful relationship. Genuine communication is not assured by talking. Listening evidences compassion and evokes communion. Listening leads to the realization of unity and lays the foundation for community. Listening is a ministry.

Listening is a way of witnessing about the gospel.

Usually we think of sharing a witness in terms of talking, repeating certain truths, offering an apology for or a defense of our religious convictions. However, in authentic witnessing, listening is just as important as speaking.

If we desire to be heard by another person, we must first be willing to hear that other person. Only in listening to the beliefs of other people do we take those people seriously and evidence the sincerity of our intent to get at the truth. Listening to the beliefs of others creates a context in which we can speak effectively about our own beliefs.

Relational experts report that our influence over other people often develops as we listen to them in ways that demonstrate our respect for their integrity. As I listen to another person sensitively, that person begins to trust me and to allow me to have an influence in his or her life.

Certainly we need never fear a confrontation between the gospel and other points of view. The truth of the gospel is sufficient for every situation. Thus, as proponents of the gospel, we hear from others in order to be heard.

Listening is the method for interpreting the Bible.

What is Bible study? Typically that term is used for the practice of reading a scriptural text and then asking what we think about it or what we can say about it. But, such an understanding is unsound. Most crucial in real Bible study is not what we think or say about a text but what that text says to us. Studying the Bible, interpreting the Bible, means listening to the Bible—really listening. In a day when there is a lot of talk about going deeper into the Word, the most fundamental need is for the Word to go deeper into us.

As long as we address the Bible, we are never challenged by it or prodded to grow because of it. We are preoccupied with our own thoughts about the text rather than oriented to hearing the text's thoughts about us. Failing to listen to the Bible, we can carry all of our biases into Bible study and perpetuate our prejudices regardless of the Bible's proclamation. We simply must learn to listen. The Bible is the Word of God, but we can miss it totally if we do not hear it attentively.

Our familiarity with the Bible often dulls our sensitivity to its message. We read a well-known passage and almost thoughtlessly assume we know it's meaning. Be careful. The Word of God leads us to salvation only as it searches us and judges us. Watch out for time-worn assumptions that blunt serious listening. What does the Decalogue's prohibition of murder say to a world that lives on the brink of nuclear annihilation and defines security in terms of weapons proliferation? What does the gospel account of Jesus feeding the five thousand people indicate about our responsibility in a hungry world? What does the parable of the Good Samaritan say to those of us who live amid racial tension? Do we allow the apostle Paul's words about the sanctity of the human body to address issues such as drug abuse and sexual promiscuity? Do we permit Christ's insistence upon a life of grace to impact our attitudes about the importance of judgment? At issue here is not what we think or say, but what the Bible declares.

Only when we listen to the Bible is the Bible a revelation to us—when we have heard it so that we are gripped by it, helped to know ourselves, informed as to what life is all about, and directed in our conduct. A biblical text becomes God's Word to us when we hear it elaborate the meaning of our lives in relation to the most fiercely contested issues in our lives. Listening is the method for interpreting the Bible.

Listening is the starting point for obeying God.

At one time I thought the Old Testament prophet Habakkuk provided a good model for attentiveness to God. However, as I read the text of the book that bears his name and listened to the words more carefully, I realized that this man offered a better example of an attitude which prohibits attention and submission to God. Look at the text.

I will take my stand to watch,
    and station myself on the tower,
and look forth to see what he will say to me, . . .

So far, so good. The words seem to ring with obedient piety. But, read on:

and what I will answer concerning my complaint.   —Habakkuk 2:1

Do you see? Habakkuk wanted God to appear only so he could dress him down, instruct the Almighty as to his dissatisfaction. He was ready to speak, but not to listen. Read on in the book and you will discover that Habakkuk did not come to obedience before God until he stood in silence and listened to God. He was confronted by the declaration and command:

But the Lord is in his Holy Temple;
    let all the earth keep silence before him.   —Habakkuk 2:20

In Romans, Paul made it clear that the ingredient essential to salvation, faith itself, comes as a result of hearing. We live the gospel only after we hear the gospel. An interesting play on words is apparent in the original language. The Greek word for hearing is *akouō* (ἀκούω). Paul wrote that the appropriate response to hearing, *akouō*, is *hypakouō* (ὑπακούω), heeding or obeying. If we intend to obey God, we must first resolve to listen to God.

Do you see? Do you understand? Listening is a profoundly important spiritual discipline that needs constant nurturing. Listening affects our relation to ourselves, to other people, and to God. We dare not ignore it or fail to practice it. In the words of Jesus, "Listen, then, if you have ears!" (Matthew 11:15).

Thanks Mary—We Needed That!

Luke 10:38-42

Two bits of reading give rise to this piece of proclamation. One is from the gospel according to Luke— a story from the ministry of Jesus that merits the attention of all of us.

Jesus had traveled to Bethany once again. As was the case on previous trips to this community, Jesus visited the household of Martha and Mary. Both ladies were glad to see Jesus, though each expressed her pleasure in a different manner.

Mary sat down at Jesus' feet—assuming the position of a learner eager to benefit from the words of her teacher. After all, Jesus did not get to their house very often. Demands upon his time were plentiful. Few people had the privilege of enjoying private moments with him. Mary was not about to miss a single word from his mouth.

Martha was different. She was equally pleased to see Jesus, but her reception took a variant form. Martha busied herself with detailed preparations to provide for what she assumed to be Jesus' needs. In fact, amid her flurry of activities, she became perturbed with Mary's inactivity. Martha even asked Jesus to join her in a reprimand of her sister.

Jesus surprised Martha with his response to her request. Lovingly he repeated her name twice—"Martha, Martha"—and then told her that she should not be so busy about so many things when only one thing was needed. On this point the biblical text allows for numerous interpretations. Either Jesus indicated that only one thing was needed or that just a few things were needed. Was Jesus telling Martha that she really needed only to listen to him or was he asking that Martha narrow her attention to only a few provisions, such as a single meal? Regardless of which textual reading is chosen, obviously Jesus was affirming the wisdom of Mary's restive attention. He was not pleased by Martha's troublesome activism and the attitude provoked by it. In essence, Jesus instructed Martha to get her priorities in order.

Just look at the wisdom contained in this narrative, the invaluable teaching of these verses.

Busyness is not synonymous with righteousness.

Culture has done a number on us. Work is considered well nigh the pinnacle of virtues. Value is defined in terms of labor. We even establish the matter of personal identity in reference to some dominant activity. Inquiries such as "Who are you?" or "Tell me about yourself" result in statements such as "I am an accountant, a farmer, an educator, a salesperson." We attempt to explain who we are by telling what we do. Most people are uncomfortable with conversations about being which do not revolve around discussions of doing.

This attitude is carried over into religion. Issues of being are swept aside by a preoccupation with doing. The question "Are you a Christian?"—an inquiry of being—is answered by a recital of labors—matters of doing: "I go to church." "I pray." "I visit the sick." Spirituality is confused with activity. Colin Morris is correct in his observation that while once we took refuge in piety to avoid the claims of action, now we take refuge in action to avoid the claims of spirituality.[1]

Like you, I am sure, I know many people whose concepts of self-importance and self-worth are determined almost exclusively by the quantity of their productivity and the extent of their activity. Often comments of self-congratulations are made to sound like complaints: "I am so busy." "I never have a spare moment." "I just work all the time." Secretly, the people behind such statements see their worth as persons wrapped up in the validity of such statements.

Be careful. Not infrequently a person so committed to ceaseless activities loses a healthy perspective on life. Priorities get distorted. Values are garbled. It is much like jogging. Many people who jog barely can talk of anything else. They enjoy discussing jogging ad infinitum, ad nauseam, every bit as much as they enjoy the running itself. Additionally they tend to look down their sweaty noses at anyone who does not run. Non-joggers are made to feel guilty because of the lack of this activity in their lives. I speak only somewhat tongue in cheek.

Martha was so busy making provisions for Jesus that she really did not devote her attention to Jesus. She worked so hard she lost her perspective—even her perspective on her work. Martha no longer realized the reason for her labor. Consequently she snapped at Mary because of her

---

[1]Colin Morris, *The Hammer of the Lord* (Nashville: Abingdon, 1973) 48.

inactivity and requested that Jesus enjoin a reprimand to get busy. Do not miss the full impact of Jesus' response to Martha.

No virtue exists in being busy. One can be breathlessly active and spiritually wrong. John Neuhaus may be exactly right in his assessment that much activism is a form of decadence.

Implicit here is the truth that being is every bit as important as doing. Christianity focuses on the quality of life not on quantity in life. Productivity is not the issue—personhood is what is important. Living as a disciple of Christ is a state of being.

In the case of Mary and Martha, Mary had chosen the better part. Quietly sitting and listening to the words of Jesus was far more important than frantically trying to provide for every perceived need of Jesus. Busyness is not synonymous with righteousness.

Life has a rhythm to it.

I do want to be careful here not to misrepresent the truth. This biblical text is no apology for inactivity, a negation of indispensable Christian action. In fact, it is not an elevation of the contemplative life to a position of religious superiority. Jesus had just told the parable of the Good Samaritan and praised ministry-oriented action.

Actually, life—particularly life in a right relationship with God—has a rhythm to it. Both rest and labor are involved—work and worship, contemplation and action.

Legend has it that on one occasion John the Evangelist was found playing with a partridge. The discoverer chided John for resting and enjoying the partridge in play rather than being busy at work. John answered: "I see you carry a bow. Why is it that you do not have it strung and ready for use?" John was told: "That would not do at all. If I kept it strung and ready for use, it would go lax and be good for nothing." "Then," John said, "Do not wonder what I do."[2] Of course, the point is that rest like work plays an important role in creation. Rest is not a diversion from labor but an ingredient in life every bit as essential as labor.

---

[2]Wayne Oates, *Confessions of a Workaholic. The Facts about Work Addiction* (New York: The World Publishing Company, 1971) 24, citing Robert Neale, *In Praise of Play* (New York: Harper & Row, 1970) 36.

Work should not be exalted above rest just as rest should not be exalted above work. A healthy life enjoys both—a consistent rhythm of involvement in each. No legitimate separation exists between be-ers and doers.

Not anything was wrong with what Martha was doing. Certainly there is a time to make preparations for a guest. Cleaning the house and fixing a meal were very much in order. The problem with Martha had to do with timing. In the presence of Jesus she needed to be still and listen to his words. A time would come again when work would be in order. But, not at the moment.

Life has a rhythm to it. Great wisdom resides in knowing when to work and when to rest, when to speak and when to listen, when to be active and when to be still.

Most essential is communion with Christ.

Here is the point of the biblical passage. The highest form of service is communion with Christ.

As one writer has noted, "We are what we belong to." Any one moment, the question is not whether we are busy or restive but whether or not we are in communion with Christ. If we belong to Christ, both our being and our doing reflect this possession.

I have learned immensely from reading the writing of a monastic named Bernardin Schellenberger. In his book entitled *Nomad of the Spirit,* Schellenberger states that "The goal of Christian spirituality is to hold to the unmistakably unique Jesus Christ and to relate to him."[3] Schellenberger goes on to point out that only through this relationship "does a person develop the strength to integrate all the fragments of his life into an organic whole and develop the kind of 'rest' that is not a question of time and leisure, but rather a question of being sustained by an ultimate meaning."[4] At issue is not activity or inactivity but relatedness—communion with Christ. And, this is a matter of morality.

Notice. The divine meaning of existence was present right there in the humble home of Martha and Mary. Martha simply needed to be still and

---

[3]Bernardin Schellenberger, *Nomad of the Spirit. Reflections of a Young Monastic,* trans. Joachim Neugroschel (New York: Crossroad, 1981) 65.
[4]Ibid.

experience it. Communion with Christ could occur. Need I say that the same potential for meaning is present here?

Well, so much for my first piece of reading. Busyness is not synonymous with righteousness. Actually life has a rhythm about it—a rhythm of work and rest. Most essential is communing with Christ.

Now for a look at the second source of the generative ideas behind today's message. A recent news item reported on the Carnegie Foundation's study of the college experience. A review of that material yields some interesting and disturbing insights.

According to the Carnegie Foundation's findings, the dominant orientation among college students today is doing. Specifically, the primary goals among students are quickly rising to the top of their chosen professions and making a lot of money. Undoubtedly such attitudes on campus reflect the spirit of our culture. But, neither bodes well for our future.

Perhaps those of us on campus acutely need to hear with clarity the words of Jesus to Martha and to heed with fidelity the model of Mary. What is the purpose of the college experience? Is it merely a time for staying busy in preparation for still more busyness? Ninety percent of those college students surveyed saw the primary purposes of these years in terms of preparation for getting jobs and making money. Only twenty-seven percent of the high school students interviewed saw the college years as a time for becoming a thoughtful citizen.

"Martha, Martha," Jesus said. . . . Substitute our names.

With his characteristic wisdom, Thomas Merton viewed the purpose of education in terms of showing persons how to define themselves authentically and spontaneously in relation to the world. In other words, the agenda within a university is a radical discovery of the self, which means a radical discovery of the self before God. College years should be devoted to listening—not just to doing, but to listening to the voice within and to the Voice from beyond. Residents of college campuses should comprise what some have called "a discernment community."

What are you doing these days? How much attention do you devote to being? And, how about listening? This is a time in your life for listening carefully for the voice of God and ordering priorities—even vocational objectives—according to his will. Nothing is more important. Nothing. If we are too busy to do that, we are way too busy.

Today, I direct your attention to Jesus' reprimand for Martha and commend for your emulation the model of Mary—Mary sitting, listening to the words of Jesus. Maybe during the potential busyness of these days your response to that commanding vision will be the same as mine: "Thanks Mary—we needed that!"

Sacramental Silence

Several years ago I was meeting with a worship committee that was making suggestions about the orders of worship for a congregation's Sunday services. During our deliberations one member of the committee mused aloud, "We need more silence in our services." Immediately I inquired as to how much silence was desired. "At least three minutes," came the very specific response. Hurriedly my mind calculated that expanse of time and considered the possibilities—what do we do about the radio broadcast, how will we handle extraneous noises, will members of the congregation be uncomfortable and restless? Suddenly I realized that along with some of the other members of the committee I was reacting negatively to the possibility of silence—a phenomenon that I appreciate. Subsequently I let down my defenses and joined in the plans to implement a three-minute period of silence during a Sunday morning service.

My guess is that my reaction to that suggestion about the possibility of silence is not totally unlike your response to the reality of silence. Evidence to that effect is the existence of our noisy world. Television provides a constant backdrop of babble in our places of residence. Radios blare in our cars. Muzak fills the elevators and waiting rooms of professional buildings. When two or more people are together, we feel a need for at least one person to be talking. We seem both to go to sleep more quickly and to wake up more easily by listening to music. Our food digests more effectively if we hear pleasant sounds as we eat it. Some even argue that they concentrate better and study more intensely surrounded by sounds. Days—maybe even weeks—come and go without any experience of silence. W. H. Auden may have been right on target when he concluded, "We are afraid of pain but more afraid of silence."

"So what?" you think. "Why deal with this particular subject in a Christian sermon? Are you on an ecological campaign against noise pollution? What is the psychological point?" Please understand that my interest in silence is not in service to a concern for better mental health, improved study habits, and the like. Silence is a spiritual discipline that can be neglected only with harmful results.

Oh, to be sure, silence is not a positive, valuable phenomenon in itself. As others have pointed out, silence may be golden or it may be just yellow. There is the silence of a graveyard and the silence of a greenhouse. The silence in a room filled with worshiping Quakers is distinctively different from the silence which pervades a room full of fatigued slumberers. Though some episodes of silence are negative phenomena to be avoided, others are positive and should be sought. My concern is for sacramental silence—silence that conveys grace, silence that nurtures the soul, silence that enriches the spirit, silence that is pregnant with positive spiritual possibilities.

I appreciate and agree with the wise counsel of the late Dag Hammarskjöld, "When all becomes silent around you, and you recoil in terror . . . do not then anesthetize yourself by once again calling up the shouts and horns . . . but gaze steadfastly at the vision until you have plumbed its depths."[1] Consider with me two forms of sacramental silence. First, the

Silence of Listening

Remember the words of T. S. Eliot in "Ash Wednesday":

Where shall the world be found, where will the word
Resound? Not here, there is not enough silence.[2]

Do you see the point? Some discoveries are unmade, some messages are unheard, some revelations are not received because of a lack of silence. Think of the spiritual implications of that one truth alone.

Silence is a necessity if we are to listen—to listen to ourselves or to others or to God. If we are always speaking or otherwise preoccupied with sounds we are unable to discern the rumblings of our own soul. Not in touch with ourselves, we become fragmented human beings. Our minds and our wills, our convictions and our emotions work at cross purposes. In order to be whole we must find time to be silent.

---

[1]Dag Hammarskjöld, *Markings,* trans. Leif Sjoberg and W. H. Auden (New York: Alfred A. Knopf, 1981) 16.

[2]T. S. Eliot, "Ash Wednesday," *Collected Poems 1909–1962* (New York: Harcourt, Brace, and World, Inc., 1963) cited in Elizabeth O'Connor, *Search for Silence* (Waco TX: Word Books, 1972) 132.

I vividly remember my days as a college student. Then as now noise was a constant companion. Friends laughed and talked loudly. Professors lectured. A cacophony of sounds reverberated down the halls of the dorm. Periodically my roommate and I got away from it all. We had a favorite place in a beautiful Tennessee state park called Natchez Trace. We would go there, rent a boat, and row our way into one of the quiet, placid coves around the shoreline. No words were spoken between us. Except for the ripple of the water lapping against the side of the boat, little else could be heard. In those moments I was renewed. I could hear myself. I could know my mind. I could be in touch with my values. My spirit soared. I do hope you have a quiet place in which you can be silent.

But it is more than a matter of personal wholeness and mental health. If we are to hear what goes on around us, there must be silence within us. Confucius said that language is like a wheel. The spokes hold the structure together, they are the syntax, but the empty spaces convey the essence of what is said.[3] How well do you hear—really hear? Ivan Illich said, "The learning of the grammar of silence is an art much more difficult to learn than the grammar of sounds."[4] You well know that very often in personal conversations what is not said, what is communicated only in silence, is often more important than what is said. If you attempt to avoid the silence, you miss the message.

Where silence becomes even more acutely important is in our relationship to God. Mother Teresa has observed that "God is the friend of silence."[5] She admonished persons to "See how nature—trees, flowers, grass grow in silence; see the stars, the moon and sun, how they move in silence."[6] This saintly lady concluded, "The essential thing is not what we say, but what God says to us and through us."[7]

Remember Elijah's experience on Mount Horeb. The prophet sought to hear the voice of God. But God was not in the uproarious noise of the wind, fire, or earthquake. The medium of divine revelation was a still small voice. Without silence it could not have been heard. Is this why Habakkuk

---

[3]Colin Morris, *The Word and the Words* (Nashville: Abingdon, 1975) 137.

[4]I. D. Illich, *Celebration of Awareness* (New York: Doubleday, 1970) cited in Morris, *The Word and the Words,* 138.

[5]Malcolm Muggeridge, *Something Beautiful for God. Mother Teresa of Calcutta* (Garden City NY: Image Books, 1977) 48.

[6]Ibid.

[7]Ibid.

was told "The Lord is in his holy temple; let all the earth keep silence before him" (2:30)? Keep in mind the observation of the psalmist:

> The heavens are telling the glory of God;
>   and the firmament proclaims his handiwork. . . .
> There is no speech nor are there words;
>   their voice is not heard;
> yet their voice goes out through all the earth,
>   and their words to the end of the world.   —Psalm 19:1, 3-4

Silence itself is a channel of divine revelation. If we are to hear the voice of God, we must still the noises that distract our attention and clog our minds.

Silence is a sacrament when through it we find health, wholeness, and grace. Do you practice the silence of listening? Consider as well the

Silence of Loving

In his autobiography, Howard Thurman described a situation in which all of the necessary words had been spoken and the persons involved were left with "the pure language of silence."[8] In reality, silence can convey what words alone cannot carry. You know the old cliché about feelings that are too deep for words. It is true. Sometimes our emotions can find their most adequate expression only through the silence of a nod, a look, a stare, a smile, or an embrace.

Martin Buber once described an interesting scene involving two men on a park bench—strangers. No word was exchanged between them. Yet each knew the other was there. Both had an attitude of openness. Buber said that in the silence of that situation profound communication occurred between these two men. Silence bore a message of care. A quiet word of dialogue happened sacramentally even though neither heard anything from the other.[9]

Sometime back I read the text of a reporter's interview with Vladimir Horowitz at age seventy-seven. The reporter asked Horowitz if he still got a kick out of applause. The old man smiled and said, "It is the silence that matters, not the applause. Anyone can have applause. But the silence, be-

---

[8]Howard Thurman, *With Head and Heart* (New York: Harcourt Brace Jovanovich, 1979) 111.

[9]Morris, *The Word and the Words*, 140.

fore and during the playing—that is everything.''[10] In the silence were an awe, a respect, an attention, a love for music that could not be conveyed by a sound. Similarly, you know of the hush that falls over an audience when the theatre curtain rises, when the performer steps on stage, when the orator moves to the lectern. In the hush is an eager anticipation—even a devotion—that cannot be stated in words.

I once heard of two friends who were to be separated by a vast expanse of geographical distance. They dreaded being cut off from each other. Finally they agreed that they would meet in silence at a particular hour each day. After several days of this experience, each concluded that distance became almost irrelevant.

Have you been in situations where speech failed, no sound was appropriate to communicate the rhythms of your spirit? Surely such a moment has come on an occasion when we have contemplated the goodness of God. Certainly such times were a part of the experience of Jesus. The apostle Paul promised that the spirit would make intercession for us when we had concerns too profound for expression in words.

How well I remember an early morning pastoral call in Louisville, Kentucky. A teenager had been killed in an automobile accident on his way to school. I did not know his parents well, but they were in need of help. When I entered their living room, I sensed a sadness, a grief, too profound for language. In that moment to have spoken would have been uncaring, obscene. The three of us simply stood in the middle of the room holding each other in a silence broken only by a muffled sobbing. More love and understanding were communicated in silence than could ever have been captured in words. Sacramental silence.

Silence is a sacrament when through it love, understanding, and grace are conveyed. Do you know the silence of loving?

I commend to you the practice of silence in a noisy world. My challenge to you is a spiritual one. Faith is involved. The discipline of silence has relevance for both the quality of our worship and the effectiveness of our ministry. Can you hear God speaking to you? You need silence—the spiritual gift of silence—in your life. The silence of which I speak is not the same as thinking about silence, learning about silence, and talking about silence. Only silence itself will suffice. So, right now, as the conclusion to this sermon, discover the sacrament of silence. Let all the earth be silent.

---

[10]*Newsweek,* 31 May 1982, 76.

Christian Life

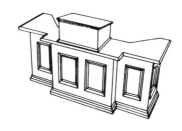

Scared to Life

John 11:38-44

A grandparent proudly related to me his observations of a grandson playing preacher. Interestingly, the little lad, not knowing that he was being watched, had decided to convene a church service while wearing a cowboy outfit. Standing behind his homemade pulpit, the young boy started to preach—choosing as his text the story of Jesus raising Lazarus from the dead. As the make-believe preacher related to his imaginary congregation the sweep of this New Testament narrative, he dramatically quoted Jesus' command at the burial cave, "Lazarus, come out." After a brief period of silence, the young boy repeated the order. With still no movement in his simulated sanctuary, the grandson lifted from his holsters two mock six-shooters and declared, "Alright, Lazarus, come out with your hands up!"

Reflections on that humorous scene have driven me to encounter a sizable amount of serious truth. The fact is that many people easily could understand it if Lazarus had wanted to stay dead. Once the agony of the unknown had been encountered, once death had been experienced, Lazarus should have been left undisturbed—so reason some. How terrible is the thought of a condemnation to life—not to be able to die. Though you may never have put the matter in just that manner, how often have you thought or spoken the words, "I could just die" or "I wish I were dead" and known that the statement was far more a stark personal confession than a casual slang expression?

All indications are that plenty of people are afraid of life—or, to use more popular terminology, scared to death. The preresurrection status of Lazarus is enviable. After all, he had died naturally, respectably. He was missed by those whom he loved, even mourned by many. At long last he was free from the hassle of life—no more dread about disease, concern about catastrophes, anxieties about vocation, or worries about family. Why did Jesus have to come along and disrupt his rest? This pervasive matter of fear requires careful attention from a biblical perspective.

The power of fear is readily documentable. Sam Keen has posited that most of the roles we play in life are motivated by fear.[1] Of course, that assessment is devoid of any value judgment. Thus, fear can be considered constructive or destructive.

Most students of fear surmise that people basically react to it in one of two ways—fight or flight. I see the first option as constructive and the second option as destructive. The research and conclusions of Bonaro Overstreet substantiate my hunch—"Of all the emotional forces that pattern our individual and interpersonal behavior, fear has the most insidious power to make us do what we ought not to do and leave undone what we ought to do."[2] Robert Frost pointed to the critical social implications of this individual reality in his statement, "There is nothing I am afraid of like scared people."[3] True, people are scared because times are dangerous. Equally true, however, is the fact that times are dangerous because people are scared.

Abnormal fear is hurtful while normal fear is helpful. Extreme fear paralyzes while more ordinary fear motivates. People who are scared to death are much more comfortable with the idea of Lazarus remaining in the tomb than with thoughts of Jesus calling Lazarus out from the grave and commissioning him to live.

Strangely enough, of all of our fears, the fear of death looms largest for most of us. To be sure, the fear of death does strange things to us. Preoccupied with fear, we may become hypochondriacs physically and cowards spiritually. Attempting to dodge fear at all costs, we cling to security with an intensity which borders on insanity. Like seeking to protect a snowball by holding it tightly in our warm hands and watching it melt, tragically many people lose completely that which they are trying to hold most tightly. To play life utterly close to the chest is never even to know life at its best. Many people are simply scared to death.

Over the past few years, I have observed carefully another type of individual. Conscientiously I have studied the behavior of people who have been in intimate scraps with death and emerged alive. A surprisingly large

[1]Sam Keen, *Beginnings Without End* (San Francisco: Harper & Row, Publishers, 1977) 57.

[2]Bonaro W. Overstreet, *Understanding Fear in Ourselves and Others* (New York: Harper & Brothers, Publishers, 1951) 3.

[3]Merrill R. Abbey, *Preaching to the Contemporary Mind* (Nashville: Abingdon Press, 1963) 24.

number of such individuals, who have faced the ultimate reality of death with some fear, walk away from that encounter with a previously unparalleled freedom to live. Precisely at the point of their critical confrontation with death, they experienced liberation both from a fear of death and from other fears as well.

William Stringfellow bore a strong witness to this striking phenomenon in a text that he prepared shortly after a close encounter with death in his life: "It is, so to speak, only then and there—where there is no equivocation or escape possible from the fullness of death's vigor and brutality, when a man is exposed in absolute vulnerability—that life can be beheld and welcomed as a gift which life is. In that singular affection for life, death is transcended in a way in which dominion is restored to a man in his own life and in his relationships with the rest of creation."[4] Later Stringfellow remarked, "It is freedom from moral bondage to death that enables a man to live humanly and to die at any moment without any concern."[5] That mentality expresses beautifully for me the opposite of being scared to death—my concept of being scared to life.

In truth, those persons who have faced death so realistically have been no closer to death than are we. Though they have received a lab report indicating the presence of malignant cells in their bodies or experienced near-fatal automobile accidents, we live within one breath of death. Thus, the crucial question for me is whether or not apart from a dramatic radicalizing scrape with death, we can know and experience the freedom to live joyously and to exercise generously a life-affirming attitude.

Of course, dealing with this question leads to discovering the role faith can play in a person's life. Authentic Christian faith provides the means by which abundant life can be experienced apart from the element of fear. Jesus invites us to lay hold of his gracious provision of abundant life.

Jesus never urged us to die for the sake of dying. Rather, his commission for us is to live for something worth dying for and to die for it if necessary. But, in such a life, death is robbed of its nature as a threat. Fear is transformed by faith—a faith that catapults us into life and instills us with a desire to wring from life every ounce of meaning possible.

---

[4]William Stringfellow, *A Second Birthday* (Garden City NY: Doubleday & Company, Inc., 1970) 67.
[5]Ibid., 203.

One of my predecessors as pastor of Broadway Baptist Church and now my good friend, J. P. Allen, likes to counsel people to walk toward their fears. How acutely wise. Here is the way to action rather than to stagnation. Acknowledge the fears in life and then place these fears in the context of faith. Subsequently, pursue life—all of it, all of it with its causes for additional fears—rather than run from it or become immobilized in it.

Can you imagine the perspective on life which was claimed by Lazarus? Note carefully the dominant characteristics in the lives of these people for whom fear is no longer a threat. I can tell you quickly what for me are some of the most attractive qualities in the lives of those for whom fear has been overcome by faith, whose goals are related to fullness of life. These are qualities to which I aspire. The first is

To speak out courageously.

How weary I have become of those sentiments that judge that every word one speaks must be carefully measured so as not to upset the apathetic or disappoint the enthusiastic. The pervasive nature of this middle-of-the-road attitude explains why so many words can be spoken with so little meaning conveyed. Once a person has looked realistically at the basic threats of life and the ultimate promises of scripture, speaking courageously should come naturally.

In Eugene O'Neill's play *Lazarus Laughed,* the emperor Caligula becomes very upset by Lazarus's resuscitation. As a matter of policy, Caligula ruled by fear. He controlled people by threatening people. As O'Neill had the emperor explain, "We must keep death dangling . . . before their eyes."[6] Lazarus presented a problem to Caligula because he removed the ultimate power by which fear was instilled and control exercised.

What a terrible travesty to lead a controlled life—forever making decisions and determining actions by sensing in which direction the wind is blowing, toward which convictions the majority of people is moving, and assessing at what cost popularity can be attained. Wayne Oates was right on target when he wrote that fear causes us to get out of earshot of our own personal integrity.[7]

---

[6]Eugene O'Neill, *Lazarus Laughed* (New York: Horace Liveright, 1927) cited in Overstreet, *Understanding Fears in Ourselves and Others,* 11.

[7]Wayne E. Oates, *Nurturing Silence in a Noisy Heart* (Garden City NY: Doubleday & Company, Inc., 1979) 103.

In recent years, the closing lines of *King Lear* have become increasingly important to me. Do you recall the comment Shakespeare placed on the lips of Edgar? ''The weight of this sad time we must obey; speak what we feel, not what we ought to say.''[8] Surely our words should be born amid our convictions and not exist as measured products of our evaluation of the conditions of acceptance and our predictions of the best path to success.

Much of the silence in today's world is an indication of individuals scared to death to speak. However, that silence can be broken. Fear can be replaced by faith. Those who are scared to death can be transformed into persons scared to life. When society's intimidations are no longer considered threats to us, we are free to speak courageously.

Also, I aspire to the ability

To claim spontaneity.

Life consists of much more than our routines. Yet, devoid of an ability to be flexible, life becomes boringly predictable, considerably less than what is possible.

Some of life's very best experiences come as surprises, interruptions, detours. Either we give ourselves to these experiences as they arise or we lose them forever. Numerous opportunities are nonrepetitive. If we do not seize their potential at the moment of their presence, we lose that promise as well as forfeit that time. Regardless of our penchant for preciseness, our preference for schedules, we simply cannot calendar spontaneity and plan for serendipity. The verbs negate the nouns.

''But what will people say?'' we ask. ''But I have so much work to be done,'' we rationalize. Quite frankly, only a brave bias toward life will release us to claim some of the best experiences in life. True wisdom is found in knowing when to work and when to play, when to stay on schedule and when to divert, when to drive forward with hard-nosed determination to accomplish certain priorities and when to recognize a higher call to loyalty that suggests a different set of priorities.

When a child is ready to take a first step, a parent cannot say, ''Wait until I finish what I am doing and I will look.'' A parent either looks at that moment or misses that glorious initiative. When a pressing wrong needs

---

[8]Peter Alexander, ed., *The Complete Works of Shakespeare* (London: Collins, 1980) 1113.

addressing, to wait is to make a serious mistake. Everyone can forgive an error made hastily in attempting to redress a wrong. But few people can forgive utter silence in the face of an unchallenged evil. Of course, we can give ourselves only to what is known, predictable, and planned but the cost involves an expensive loss of wonder, excitement, and love.

Speaking of love, whoever heard of real love taking action on the basis of calculations of liabilities and assets, deciding a direction by slide-rule measurements of possibilities and problems? Henri Nouwen conveys the truth in his comments, "Real love says, 'forever.'. . . Love comes from that place within us where death cannot enter. Love does not accept the limits of hours, days, weeks, months, years, or centuries. Love is not willing to be imprisoned by time."[9] The New Testament says that perfect love drives out all fear (1 John 4:18).

Of course, risk is involved in such a life-style. But, is not risk inherent in reality? Without risk life becomes a terrible bore devoid of spontaneity. Those persons who have encountered the ultimate threats of this life and eradicated them by an exercise of faith are no longer scared to death but scared to life. They claim spontaneity.

I aspire as well

To accept challenges gladly.

Raymond Brown offered a disturbing observation about some of his students. This beloved professor of mine wrote of students who had allowed fear to restrict their pursuit of truth. His exact words were, "So fearful were they that they would lose Christ, they never really ventured to find him. Afraid he would become smaller, they never really learned how big he really is."[10]

The principle is applicable generally. Accepting a challenge gladly is the difference between being scared to death and being scared to life. We can be so afraid of illness that we never enjoy health. Or, we can determine that life is too short not to live every moment to its fullest. We can be so afraid of criticism that we never do anything that merits criticism, or af-

---

[9]Henri J. M. Nouwen, *A Letter of Consolation* (San Francisco: Harper & Row, Publishers, 1982) 32.

[10]Raymond Bryan Brown, *The Fire of Truth,* ed. Richard A. Spencer (Nashville: Broadman Press, 1982) 85.

firmation. Conversely, we can accept criticism for what it is and live to such an extent that criticism is a compliment. We can be so fearful of failure that we never even attempt to succeed at anything. On the other hand, we can prefer failure in a noble effort to the moral embarrassment of no effort at all.

Numerous voices in today's world instruct us regarding a mass fear of nuclear war. That fear can go either way— paralysis which is synonymous with bondage or an engagement with critical issues in the international community as an expression of freedom. A fear of war can result in efforts for peace. A fear of crime can result in a pursuit of justice. A fear of loneliness can issue forth in a search for community. Crucial is whether or not fear has encountered faith and found an orientation to life.

A comment from Martin Luther King, Jr. has had continuing benefit for me. One night in Montgomery, Alabama, when fatigue and faltering courage were almost overwhelming realities in his life, a wise old black lady sensed the situation and counseled the civil-rights leader. She said straightforwardly, "I don told you we is with you all the way . . . but even if we ain't with you, God's gonna take care of you." [11] To me, King's response was every bit as important as the woman's wisdom. He wrote, "As she spoke these consoling words, everything in me quivered and quickened with a pulsing tremor of raw energy." [12] That is it! That is an indication of one who is scared to life.

Words which became meaningful to King on that occasion have retained meaning for me until this day:

Fear knocked at the door.
Faith answered.
There was no one there. [13]

My much-cherished, now-departed colleague L. D. Johnson put me in touch with a wonderful story from the early Christian community which epitomizes this whole matter. In the second and third centuries numerous Christians were driven underground by a hostile Roman government. They were consigned to the Numidian mines of North Africa. Branded on their brows with a red-hot iron, chained so that they could not stand quite up-

---

[11]Martin Luther King, Jr. *Strength to Love* (New York: Harper & Row, Publishers, 1963) 117.

[12]Ibid.

[13]Ibid.

right, frequently having their eyes gouged out, these people were forced
to live out their days underground. Here and there on smooth rocks, pa-
thetic messages scribbled in charcoal recorded their presence. Some had
prayed for sympathy or asked to be remembered. Others had recorded the
suffering and separation from their families. But the most frequent inscrip-
tion, reiterated in what appeared to be a frenzy of hope was "vita, vita,
vita."[14] Life! Life! Life! That was it—persons of faith scared to life.

My challenge to you in this sermon is an invitation to live—to live so
as to fear only what should be feared and to overcome in faith all of the
other fears of our lives so that we can know personally courage, spontaneity, and gladness. Then, when Jesus calls our names, as he called forth
Lazarus, we can come running. As we dash from the tombs constructed by
prior fears and scurry toward life, no doubt we will hear again and understand at even deeper levels the meaning of the angelic refrain which was
sung at Christ's birth, and which resounds through all generations, "Fear
not!" (Luke 2:10).

Indeed, fear not!

---

[14]L. D. Johnson, *The Morning after Death* (Nashville: Broadman Press, 1978)
136.

It's Your Signboard

One morning when I lived in Texas I had to take a guest to the Dallas-Fort Worth Airport to catch an early flight. The timing was such that my trip back to the office was slowed considerably and even stopped periodically by the crunch of rush-hour traffic. During one of the complete stops, my sleepy eyes focused on a huge billboard erected near the expressway. The huge expanse of space was empty except for the telephone number of the owner who obviously wanted to rent the space to someone.

When I saw the phone number I did a double take and then immediately tried to remember the phone number at my office. Either that number on the signboard was the same as my office number or one digit was out of sequence. The more I thought about the two numbers the more confused I became. Then, suddenly, my thoughts shifted completely. "What if this is my signboard? What if this massive amount of space is mine to do with as I wish, to write on as I choose? What would I most like to say to all of those who pass by here and look at it?"

Now let me toss that hypothetical question to you. What if you discovered that you own a billboard by a busy expressway? The printed telephone number of the owner is your phone number. At your disposal is a vast amount of space viewed daily by thousands of people and monthly by millions. You can use this billboard as a giant pulpit from which to convey to the community any message you choose. What would you write there? What do you most want to say to the largest audience possible? You can convey any message you desire to write. So, what will it be . . . ?

Jesus Saves
The Wages of Sin is Death
Where's the Beef?
Repent
Prayer Makes a Difference
You Are Somebody
Go For It
I'm O.K., You're O.K.

Grace
Peace
Tithe Now
Hang In There
Joy
Justice
You Can Make It
Someone Cares

Think about it carefully. If such a signboard is yours, what would you place on it?

Very likely the statement you would choose to placard before society would offer an insight into your needs personally. Almost instinctively each of us would be inclined to say to others what we most need to hear for ourselves.

Of course, a few exceptions are possible. If we are feeling really disgusted with everybody and everything we just might write "Get Lost," "Perish!" If we are weary of the hassle of interpersonal relationships, we could just put in huge print "Buzz Off. Leave Me Alone." If we are mad at everybody and generally disgruntled with the world, here is a chance to let it be known. The signboard could read "I Hate Everybody." Such exceptions are based on our need to say something rather than on our need to hear something.

Those possibilities aside, generally we will try to communicate to others what we want someone to communicate to us. If we need to hear a word of love, we might just spell love in bold red letters. Red would be best, would it not? If we are anxious about peace, we can set that word before the eyes of all who look in that direction. Maybe we could paint a dove beside the word. The point is that if you have a signboard at your disposal, what you place on it will provide an insight into your own needs. What would you write on your signboard?

Additionally, what you choose to write or to picture for all of the world to see will be indicative of the kind of gospel in which you believe. If you are forced to reduce your statement to society to the number of words easily readable on a billboard, you will be driven to state what you perceive to be most basic about the gospel. Will you communicate to others promise or threat, indictment or encouragement, hope or harangue? Will your message help make someone's day or break it?

When I lived in Nashville, Tennessee, each afternoon my drive home took me past a billboard rented by a local church in the city. Though I do not remember all of the words posted there, I do recall the concept of the gospel which was stated. The center of attention was the picture of a dead man in a casket. To the side of that morbid portrait was a statement about judgment and underneath it an invitation to the church which had rented the signboard. One look at that sign by the expressway revealed the basic gospel perception of that congregation. Here was an unmistakable announcement about a faith preoccupied with avoiding judgment and preparing for death.

What primal concept of the gospel will you present? It's your signboard. What will you write on it? Undoubtedly your response to these questions will provide a profound insight into your basic understanding of the gospel. Is it good news or bad news? Is it about death or life? What do you say?

By this point in the sermon you well may be wondering how such fanciful questions as these could have any relation at all to worship generally, much less to Christian proclamation particularly. Please stay with me a bit longer. I believe something extremely important is at stake here. That weird-named Old Testament prophet Habakkuk indicated as much.

Most people catch sight of the gospel at a glance. Understanding is shaped by a composite of convictions gathered by means of glimpses. Few people take time to stop and talk theology. Seldom is there an opportunity to sit and chat leisurely about a gospel-informed philosophy of life. Our witness is not so much a monologue carefully heard as it is an impression quickly made in passing.

Great wisdom is involved in the divine suggestion offered to Habakkuk concerning an effective sharing of his vision. One translation reads, "Write down clearly on tablets what I reveal to you, so that it can be read at a glance" (2:2 TEV). Other translations make more explicit the idea of writing the message so that it can be read by those who are running. Habakkuk had a billboard-like decision to make. So do we.

Obviously, if conclusions about our priorities and commitments are formed on the basis of occasional quick glances at our signboards, we are challenged to speak or write clearly. If our signboards are in reality the events of our lives, we are challenged to live consistently—to incarnate the gospel at every moment so others can see it at any moment.

Here is the crux of the matter. We do own a signboard—every one of us. Like it or not, we do make a statement, bear a witness about ourselves and the kind of gospel in which we believe. And remember, what is seen is viewed at a glance—catching an impression of us under the pressure of finals, seeing us react to a bad call by a referee in an intramural game, observing our response to someone who just backed a truck into our car, noting how we handled a compliment or maybe a criticism. No one hangs around long enough to listen to our explanation of why we did what we did or why we said what we said. People just take note of us, form an opinion about us, and move on. No opportunity is provided for efforts at simplicity or complexity, only for insights into reality. "Write . . . clearly . . . so that it can be read at a glance."

In his *Theopoetic,* Amos Wilder said that "human nature and human societies are more deeply motivated by images and visions than by ideas; by experiences more than by dogmas."[1] The phone number on the billboard is your number. So, what word do you write, what vision do you depict? How will you motivate others?

If the counsel of Habakkuk is to be trusted, and it is, the statement we make ought to be related to the quality of life. In the case of the prophet, an attempt was made to instruct people on the nature of righteousness, that is, the nature of the good life. Using a phrase short enough for a bumper sticker, Habakkuk said, "The just shall live by his faith" (2:4 KJV). Students of this text know that the issue was not faith as a matter of stagnant belief but faith in terms of dynamic faithfulness. Really righteous people live in faithfulness to God. That was Habakkuk's redeeming vision received from God to be passed on to people hurrying by.

What is our vision? What is the counsel we place before others by means of our signboards? The activities of our lives? Do we encourage negativism or pass on pessimism? Is the vision we commend one of distrust or disgust or what? We can major on the bare minimums of life, what is needed just to get by, or we can commend maximum life, life so filled with abundance as to be made eternal. In whatever space we have for addressing whatever glance comes our way we can strike out at lostness and despair or we can lift people's sights to redemption and hope.

You recognize by now that I am interpreting my encounter with an empty signboard and Habakkuk's experience with writing tablets as parables— parables about our lives. We are walking billboards. We do communicate more incidentally than we may ever attempt intentionally.

---

[1]John H. Westerhof III and John D. Eusder, *The Spiritual Life. Learning East and West* (New York: The Seabury Press, 1982) 45.

Passersby see us or listen to us and form a conclusion about us and the gospel to which we are committed. What do they see or hear—encouragement or discouragement, anger or joy, promise or reprimand, defeat or victory, bad news or good news?

Incidentally, later in that day on which I made the early morning trip to the airport, I checked my phone number at the office and compared it with the phone number on the signboard. Sure enough, the numbers were the same except for sequence. The signboard was not mine. It belonged to someone else. But thoughts about it had been helpful and an important realization had resulted—that signboard is not mine, but I do have one and I must place on it consistently and clearly what best states my conviction about the gospel and life.

Yes, and you have a signboard too. Each of us has a signboard and a word from God about the use of it, "Write . . . clearly . . . so that it can be read at a glance . . . those who are righteous will live because they are faithful to God." So, what is on your signboard? What have you placed there or what are you placing there for all to see?

A Visit to Jesus' Cafe

On the south end of Main Street in Fort Worth, Texas, there is a place called "Jesus' Cafe." A battered old sign hanging tenuously over an unimpressive, rundown building caught my eye one afternoon. The first time I saw it, I did a double take—"Jesus' Cafe." Then, of course, I realized the nature of the establishment—it is a Mexican restaurant owned by someone named Jesús. However, if passersby do not know the ethnic makeup of that neighborhood and the proper Spanish pronunciation of "Jesús," they well could assume the place is called "Jesus' Cafe."

Because that building is located on the street that leads to a major hospital in the city, I passed by it at least once every week in the course of pastoral visitation. Consequently, after discovering the place, on numerous occasions I allowed by mind to toy with various possibilities related to my initial misreading of the sign.

A seemingly endless series of questions has come to mind, followed quickly by some intriguing potential answers. What if the place really is Jesus' cafe—a cafe run by the Jesus whom we meet in the New Testament? What would that be like? Would I want to go there? Definitely, I would want to go there. By all means, yes. I would want to visit the place often. In fact, in my imagination, I have visited Jesus' Cafe. Allow me, please, to illustrate my personal speculation about that visit—thoughts that hopefully contain some substantive instruction and application for all of us.

What about the food in Jesus' Cafe?

My guess is that every item on the menu is good for a person. According to the apostle Paul, a person's physical body is considered to be the temple of God. Surely, if that is true, Jesus views the body in that same manner. Thus, undoubtedly, he does not make available food that is harmful rather than healthy.

Perhaps the menu prepared by Jesus does not provide everything we want. But, most likely, it does contain everything we need. As you well know, discerning and accepting the difference between what we want and what we need are in themselves steps toward good health. Maybe if more people allowed their appetites to be shaped by their real needs, all of us would be better off.

Interestingly enough, my mind did not linger for long on the menu— how many dishes are available, how many courses are provided. For some reason, in Jesus' Cafe, the food did not seem to matter all that much.

Well, what about the price of the food?

No doubt some people are surprised by that question. A few individuals even may argue that any talk of economics is irrelevant to faith. I disagree respectfully. Costs are associated with the food provided. Jesus never advocated a philosophy of something for nothing per se. In fact, Paul, a disciple of Jesus, jolted a group of pseudopietists out of their laziness, which they tried to pass off as spirituality, by suggesting that if they did not get to work they should cease to eat. Yes, the food has prices on it.

Please do not misunderstand, though, no person in Jesus' Cafe is allowed to go hungry merely because of an inability to pay the price of a meal. Jesus cares infinitely more for the worth of a person than for the market value of a piece of bread. The one who taught his disciples a basic prayer of only sixty-five words or so, depending on the way the Greek is translated, devoted seven of those words to a request for food—our daily bread.

The prices on the various food items in Jesus' Cafe represent descriptions of value, not absolute restrictions on availability. I do not believe a person ever leaves that place malnourished or hungry because of unemployment, a lack of initiative, some form of poor health, or bondage within the vicious cycle of poverty. No. More than once the thought has entered my mind that Jesus must view access to food as an inalienable human right!

Another question. What about the service in Jesus' Cafe?

Incredible! What else can I say about it? No newspaper reporter visiting the establishment in order to write a published review of it would believe her eyes.

What is so interesting is that most of the time you cannot tell who are the customers and who are the waiters and waitresses. From the time a person enters the place until that individual departs, everyone appears eager to help, to serve. Ironically, when unknown individuals enter the establishment for the first time, in contrast to most other places, in Jesus' Cafe they receive even more attention than others. The regulars seem anxious to see to it that no one feels strange or out of place there. All exhibit a desire to cause a person who comes there once to return again and again.

I know that some people will find it hard to believe what I'm going to say next. But, speaking of service, it is a fact. Sometimes while people are eating or just sitting and talking, individuals come up to them and offer to wash their feet. You never have seen service like that which takes place there.

O.K., but what about the atmosphere of the place?

That is a good question. I know some people who are very picky about a restaurant's "feel" or ambiance.

I must warn you that Jesus' Cafe frequently is filled with a lot of loud talk and raucous laughter. Every once in a while you might hear an outburst of profanity, though invariably that is followed with a hush soon broken by an apology. People just get so excited about telling their individual stories and sharing their concerns that sometimes an inappropriate word comes out to reveal a very appropriate emotion.

A strange blend of intensity and lightheartedness is sensed in Jesus' place. At one table people may be talking about political reform and at another spiritual revival. Often I have seen a man weeping openly on one side of the room while on the other a woman was singing "hallelujah." You get the idea that all of the topics for conversation take this world and its events very seriously, but not ultimately so. In fact, not anything about the place conveys the idea that it or we will exist in this location forever. Strangely, even the dialogues which sound so serious have about them an air of enviable lightness.

I suppose that visitors to Jesus' Cafe are most impressed by the unmistakable evidences of personal interest displayed in them. Everyone moves about with sensitivity, seeking to be assured that everyone else is satisfied. As you might imagine, that creates an unparalleled atmosphere, a warm, hospitable, comforting, peaceful environment.

The fact is that people who come to Jesus' Cafe regularly appear much more committed to talking, visiting, and enjoying fellowship than to eating. Thus, the place has an atmosphere conducive to comfort if not enjoyment. Naturally, then, that raises the question of

What kind of people go there?

Well, you would have to see it personally to believe it fully. Invariably gathered in Jesus' Cafe is the most unlikely crowd of people anyone possibly could imagine.

Sitting at the same table talking to each other intently as friends are a man who has been in prison and a woman who spends the most of her time involved in the ministry of a local church. I really do not know how some of the people ever got there. Usually, on almost any day, you can see people on crutches, individuals with serious physical maladies, and persons who are obvious social misfits. Racial origin is no barrier to interpersonal fellowship there. Why, I have seen such diverse people gathered at the same dinner table that the scene reminded me of a United Nations conference.

As you have undoubtedly guessed by now, there is no dress code in Jesus' Cafe. In fact, people do not seem to pay much attention to each other's attire. Hard-hat-wearing construction workers sit talking to bank presidents outfitted in three-piece pin-striped suits. Arm in arm walk ladies whose dresses come from Saks Fifth Avenue, K-Mart, and Goodwill.

When you look over the crowd of people, you may arrive at the same idea I hold. These folks never would have gotten together had it not been for Jesus' Cafe. In fact, an experience with Jesus is the only thing they hold in common. But, astonishingly, that is enough.

One final note of interest,

Would you go back there again?

Would I return to Jesus' Cafe? My goodness, yes. I do not believe I could keep from returning to that place. So much more happens there than merely the eating of a meal. In fact, the sense of fullness one receives there is totally disproportionate to what one eats. Admittedly, though, it is a different kind of fullness.

While there, inevitably remarkable things happen. Somehow sorrows get comforted, burdens lightened, fears relieved. Even if a person arrives there fatigued from the work of the day, depressed by the troubles of the world, and disturbed by the prospects of tomorrow, before leaving Jesus' Cafe, the person will have a handle on how to cope with difficulties and maybe even an idea on how to solve some staggering problems.

Quite honestly, when I am there my spirit soars. My soul is refreshed. I do not know if it is the place, the food, the conversation, or just what, but I leave that place with a sense of well-being internally, with a vibrant hope for peace internationally, and with the firm conviction that justice is a real possibility.

Yes, I would go back again and again. My only wish is that the crowd there would pick up a bit, that more people would discover the place. That's strange. Though in a sense I would like for the number of regulars to remain comfortably small and the place a kind of personal hideaway, something within me impels my telling others about it. I do hope I can convince some of my friends to try it. I know they will like it.

Referring to liking something, perhaps by now you are not liking this speculation, maybe you are even more than a little put out by all of this imagination. Questions may have come to your mind, inquiries like, "Has he lost his senses? How could he envision such descriptions? Is not this fantasy distantly removed from the gospel of Christianity?"

Let me commend to you those passages in the Gospels which speak of our eating together—fellowship in the kingdom, attendance at a great Messianic banquet, breaking and eating a loaf of bread while sipping from a cup in unity, sharing a meal both now and in eternity. Could it be, is it possible, that Jesus wants things to be that way now? Surely not. But there is that rickety old sign on Main Street in Fort Worth—Jesus' Cafe—and there are those intriguing, gripping passages in the Gospels—Jesus as Bread. I do not know. I really do not know. Maybe Jesus does want things that way, desire that life be lived in such a manner, now. Maybe he does.

What do you think?

Mad as Heaven

"Be angry, and sin not!" (Ephesians 4:26 KJV) Far more than a mere suggestion of wise counsel from some unknown ancient writer, that admonition carries the force of an authoritative moral mandate from the inspired word of God. "Be angry, and sin not!" Need I tell you how tough that is? Do you wonder if faithful obedience to such a maxim is possible?

Pay close attention to this biblical passage. The presence of anger is not indicative of sin. Surely that realization is a relief to a lot of us. To experience anger is not wrong in itself. Any moral verdict on anger must take into account both its motivation and its expression.

In reality, not to experience anger in our world can be more morally reprehensible than to experience it. How can a sensitive, conscientious person live where we live and not be angry?

I watch news reports of a city leveled by a tornado. The camera catches graphically the pillage of nature and then focuses on looters ransacking stores in shambles. I get mad. How can people be so callous as to take advantage of businesses already decimated by disaster? Then I realize that some of those folks scurrying away with stolen items never had another opportunity to shop for what they wanted. Only amid illegality and chaos can they do what others do respectably, enjoy amid law and order. Anger arises over a system that builds in measures by which the rich get richer and the poor get poorer. After all, no poor people possess discount cards which make available warehouse items at wholesale prices or profit from contacts in industry that can result in considerable cost reductions in all kinds of materials. High-interest income is reserved for people with money to invest.

I study the expenditures of the federal budget alongside a look at the priorities of various international economic systems. If only a small portion of the funds now dedicated to armaments could be channeled into food production and distribution, no one—*no one*—would have to go hungry. I get mad.

At times my anger is less rational. On numerous occasions I have walked away from postsurgical conversations in hospital rooms and found myself angry at cancer cells in young bodies, mad at crippling diseases destroying bright, strong minds. Such general anger sometimes becomes very specific and intensely personal. A young man with a brilliant future botches it needlessly with a nonsensical criminal act. A beautiful, talented coed confronted by all kinds of good options for the future, gets drunk, gets in a car, and kills a lot of the future as well as the person behind the wheel of the car she struck. I get mad.

Of course, not all of my anger is so noble. A good bit of it fails to qualify as the expression of an offended conscience, a matter of morality. I get mad when people take advantage of me, gossip about me, and try to run over me. More often than I like to admit, in simple selfishness, I get angry because I do not get what I want. Such anger is the product of my humanity.

Most often what my anger does to me is worse than what it does to other people. I somewhat identify with an experience related by my friend Barry Bailey. A man driving home late one night took a shortcut and on it had a flat tire. At 1:00 in the morning, he discovered that his jack did not work. Looking down the strange road, he saw a dark farmhouse. He hated to awaken the people who lived there, but maybe they owned a jack. The man started walking toward the house. As he stepped along through the night, his mind took over. These were his thoughts: "I'm probably going to make that man mad by knocking on his door at this late hour. Likely, I will awaken him from his sleep. Even if he does own a jack, probably he will be so furious with me that he will not let me use it." He reached the farmhouse and knocked on the door. When the farmer opened the door to meet him, the motorist shouted in his face: "Keep your old jack!"[1]

"Be angry and sin not!" Paul, or whoever wrote Ephesians, might just as well have left off the first words. Anger is a given—sometimes the best evidence that we are human, sometimes the most immediately visible expression of our compassion. Anger is a predictable fire in our minds and emotions. No one has to tell us to kindle it. In question is what we are to do with it—whether or not we harness anger as an energetic heat and guiding light or allow ourselves to be burned up by it.

---

[1]Barry Bailey, *Living with Your Feelings* (Nashville: Abingdon, 1980) 28.

Quite frankly, I talk to a lot of people regularly who tell me that they are "mad as hell." Actually, they do not have to spell it out. I can hear the anger in their voices, sense it in their dispositions, and see it in their physical actions. Probably I recognize such anger so quickly because I know it so intimately. From time to time their experience is mine.

When I encounter that kind of anger, red flags go up in my mind. Fear sends a chill down my spine. Not anything good can come from a person "mad as hell." Most likely the result of such a disposition will be the fury of hell conveyed indiscriminately. Relationships will be harmed, individuals injured, emotions gutted, and problems proliferated. Anger will give way to sin.

In Ephesians, the writer outlined an alternative—"be angry and sin not." This was his way of telling us to set our anger in the context of our faith, to condition our expressions of anger by the gifts of love and grace. What the writer of Ephesians commended, I have chosen to describe as being "mad as heaven."

Please do not confuse my words with counsel for weakness born out of timidity. Do not hear me encouraging a repression of anger. Do not think me unrealistic. Be angry—I need not tell you that. You will get there on your own. Be angry, but do not sin. That is the point. Here is the reason for talking about heaven.

What is the difference between being "mad as hell" and "mad as heaven"? What distinguishes acceptable anger from unacceptable anger? How can anger be expressed responsibly? What kind of anger befits a Christian? I know the questions well—better than the answers. However, allow me to take a stab at some responses.

Anger that is disciplined, not reckless

That is the wrath of moral wisdom. As you might suspect, temper tantrums do not have a place here. What is left once anger has been ventilated by shouting, throwing things, and heaving about? A mess—a difficult-to-clean-up mess in more ways than one. Words recklessly hurled about can be even more dangerous than flying hats, golf clubs, and other items furiously tossed into the air.

Our terminology may be significant. We speak of a person "getting mad" and "throwing a fit"—a good choice of words, really. No reason is involved. No discipline is exercised. Chaos is created.

Ironically, anger is encouraged and prolonged by such fitful behavior rather than dissipated by it. Picture an enraged bull in the proverbial china shop and you will catch something of the situation involved. One expression of anger creates conditions that precipitate more anger. A cycle of anger develops. When out of control, anger is closely related to the fury of hell.

"Be angry, and sin not." The presence of anger does not excuse an absence of reason or a neglect of discipline. Being mad need not, must not, coincide with ceasing to think. Chaotic emotions personally will result in chaotic conditions socially. Needed is

Anger that is constructive, not destructive

That, by the way, is the second distinctive I will mention. To be mad as heaven is to act so as to build up, not to tear down.

Though I do not wish to make an appeal to selfishness in order to commend constructive anger, the truth is that destructive anger ultimately does more harm to the person harboring it than to those considered objects of it. If your anger will not rest apart from attack and destruction, eventually you will achieve your goal—but you will be victim as well as victor.

Destructive anger ignores all limits. Everything and everyone can be destroyed—including the person who is mad. Furiously flailing away at all people and things, taking cheap shots at self-designated opponents, and working to wreak havoc in institutions of disfavor may provide an immediate emotional release, but the cost has to be paid by a sacrifice of integrity, a compromise of compassion—ultimately a dissipation of self-worth. Angry persons bent on the destruction of others ultimately find themselves destroyed by their primary motivation.

Ponder the model of Jesus. A part of what he saw at the Temple made him angry. Jesus vented his wrath. He let the people know he was mad. Those individuals who were trying to make money off religious devotion were driven out of the Temple precincts by Jesus. Why? Did he intend to be destructive? No. The goal of Christ was constructive action—the restoration of a place of prayer.

I know plenty of people who are "mad as hell" at agencies, institutions, churches, and other individuals. So long as that is their plight, we can anticipate from them little more than a destructive fight. A better way does exist, however. We need

Anger that is aimed at reconciliation, not alienation

That is the third characteristic of a positive anger.

In the Jewish mind, sunset marked the beginning of a new day. Thus, the writer of Ephesians counseled his readers to deal with their anger before sunset. Any day of anger was to be also a day of reconciliation. No extension of space—chronological or personal—was considered healthy. Anger required attention when experienced.

The potential for anger is most prevalent in the very relationships that are most intimate. Thus, within the family—particularly within the family—the work place, and the worship center, anger is predictable. This anger will find expression. The goal of it is crucial. If the energy fired by anger can be channeled into efforts dedicated to unity, good can come from it. If not, little good is possible. Hellish anger divides and separates—does exactly what you would expect; perpetrates the very essence of hell—causes alienation.

What are we to do? A temptation toward alienation is terribly strong. When angry, typically we want to stalk off by ourselves, to strike out at others, and to stop all communication. What kind of anger can work to effect reconciliation?

Anger that embraces forgiveness, not retaliation

That is the last distinctive I will mention.

If a person is bent on getting even with someone, paying someone back, making others rue the day they did wrong, forget it. Evil prevails. Hell wins. But, another way is possible.

To be sure, the alternative is not easy. We take a certain delight in striking back, getting even. Perhaps that is why Frederick Buechner has said that of the seven deadly sins, anger is the most fun.[2] Remember, though, that the laughter is shortlived and the satisfaction does not last.

Forgiveness is essential. Anger and forgiveness can live together. One does not negate the other. In a very fine book on forgiveness, Lewis Smedes teaches us that we are not failures in forgiveness because we continue to be angry about some painful wrong done to us. Anger is understandable.

---

[2]Frederick Buechner, *Wishful Thinking. A Theological ABC* (San Francisco: Harper & Row, Publishers, 1973) 2.

But in the presence of forgiveness, anger is affected by forgiveness. Eventually forgiveness destroys the malice in anger and, as Smedes comments, "Anger minus malice gives hope."[3]

To be mad as heaven is to live in hope of a better day. Actions of such anger are disciplined and constructive. Relationships are not terminally ruptured by it. In fact, reconciliation is often experienced because forgiveness is practiced.

But, hear this. These words cannot be heeded simply or easily. This sermon offers no quick fix of healthy anger, some easy therapy for the masses. To be mad as heaven requires being in touch with heaven.

Look once more at the Ephesians passage. Positive anger is the experience of persons changed by the presence of God in their lives and aware of their membership in the fellowship of faith. This command about anger from the writer of Ephesians came in the context of a discussion about conversion—the enumeration of qualities that characterize the lives of God's people. Hear this. People bent on mastering the emotion of anger by themselves will fail. But, hear this as well. God's help is as available as it is essential!

"Be angry, and sin not."

---

[3]Lewis B. Smedes, *Forgive and Forget: Healing the Hurts We Don't Deserve* (San Francisco: Harper & Row, Publishers, 1984) 109.

What Bothers You?

What, if anything, bothers you? I mean, what really bothers you? What is it that almost instantaneously will incite a rampage of joy in your emotions, that suddenly will prompt you to set aside everything that interferes with celebration, that invariably will cause you to run and shout or to dance and sing?

What, if anything, bothers you? Do you have a capacity for indignation? What will so offend your conscience that you act on it, so prick your anger that you unleash it, so nauseate your sense of decency that you explode with a negation of it? What, if anything, bothers you?

I am well aware that the counsel of our culture runs counter to the purpose for which these questions are raised. Suave sentiments, unruffled emotions, are widely acclaimed behavioral models. Enthusiasm is out. Coolness is in. You know the strategy: "Take everything in stride. Don't show your hand. Face life as an unaffectable poker player." Neither shouts of happiness nor sobs of sadness are welcomed. "Be mature." Too much crying or laughing makes people uncomfortable. Spontaneous displays of emotion draw frowns. Only carefully programmed revelations of feelings of any kind are acceptable.

Do you see the radical contradiction between our present predicament, which ultimately breeds a deadly apathy, and the biblical situation, which vibrates with lively, actional intensity? Take as examples the two New Testament passages upon which this sermon is based. In one instance, Jesus applauded an extravagant display of devotion on the part of—from the disciples' point of view—a very questionable woman. Jesus was pleased that sacrificial love had touched off a response that could not be contained by convention or controlled by cold reason. Leave it to Judas and his kin to question such an act of unconditional commitment and to figure out more "appropriate" ways to express love. The Lord liked it and promised that this woman's behavior would be remembered wherever the gospel is proclaimed.

In the other instance, Jesus himself demonstrated emotions unbound. He had had it with those who prostituted religious rituals for personal gain and compromised a house of worship for purposes of commerce. Thus, he acted. With whip in hand, he freed the caged birds and the animals and sent the group of self-serving scoundrels scurrying.

How do you see yourself in relation to those two New Testament stories? Would you ever act in such a manner—either positively or negatively, joyously or angrily? What, if anything, bothers you?

Consider the question positively.

The Bible is filled with accounts of people who, moved by love or devotion, sang spontaneously, shouted out loudly, wept openly, and acted impulsively. Remember how Mary the mother of Jesus could not repress a song of joy once she heard the angelic announcement regarding the birth of the Savior? Think of the small-statured but dignified Roman official Zacchaeus who wanted so badly to see this Jesus that he scaled a tree. You really cannot climb a tree with much dignity! Imagine the apostle Peter fishing out on the lake with his peers, then suddenly recognizing the risen Lord and desiring so much to be by his side that he dove into the water and swam to the shore.

What bothers you, positively speaking? For what or for whom will you set aside all reservations, pull out all the stops, and let go completely? I think of those lines from Wordsworth in "Lines Composed a Few Miles Above Tintern Abbey":

> . . . And I have felt
> A presence that disturbs me with the joy
> Of elevated thoughts; . . . [1]

Have you ever been disturbed by joy? Are you capable of it? Can you ever care so much that you act without a calculation of what people will think, apart from speculation on possible consequences?

I like the story, whether apocryphal or true, of the professor who came to class one beautiful day and stood for a long while gazing out the window

---

[1]William Wordsworth, lines 93-95 of "Lines Composed a Few Miles Above Tintern Abbey," *Wordsworth. Poetry and Prose,* ed. W. M. Merchant (Cambridge: Harvard Press, 1967) 154, cited in Raymond Bryan Brown, *The Fire of Truth,* ed. Richard A. Spencer (Nashville: Broadman Press, 1982) 88.

at a landscape being transformed by budding trees, flowering plants, and greening grass. Finally, the man turned to his students and announced with a smile while leaving the room, "I have a rendezvous with spring."

Oh, I know the possible critique. "Life can't be sustained with such irresponsibility. That man had a contract to teach. Students were present for his lecture. How can an educational institution survive such questionable whims of the spirit?" I know. I know! Surely, that is right. But, how can institutions survive and life persist with meaning apart from some recognition that at times a person's spirit must defy convention by means of emotions capable of extravagance?

On more than one occasion, Jesus pictured salvation, life in the kingdom of God, as a goal and a life-style that compel excess. Why, entering the kingdom was likened to a man finding a pearl of great price, discovering a gem for which he had searched for a lifetime. Once found, ownership of that prize took precedence over all else. With others looking on cynically, the man hurriedly, enthusiastically sold all his earthly goods in order to purchase that pearl. Or again, a woman had lost a cherished coin. Schedules stopped dead still. Cooking, mending, visiting, working had to wait. Feverishly, singlemindedly, excitedly the woman looked for the coin until it was found.

What bothers *you*? For what will you labor feverishly? For what will you forego schedules? A presence that disturbs with joy, a rendezvous, a pearl of great price—what? For God's sake, what? What will drive you to worship, to service, to devotion? What bothers you?

Consider the question negatively.

At what point do you get incensed enough to act? What disturbs your conscience to such an extent that you can no longer rest? How much wrong does it take to make you work to correct it? When does your tolerance of the unreligious, irreligious, or sacrilegious terminate?

Moses had watched a situation fraught with evil for years. But, one day he saw a slave beaten and something inside him snapped and he became a new Moses. You cannot understand the patriarch apart from that moment. What would it take for you? Amos reached the boiling point when he saw rich people taking advantage of poor people and superficially religious folks using their religion for personal gain. Prophecy spewed out of his mouth. What is your boiling point?

When have you had enough? What will trigger a significant moral response from your latent moral convictions—a lie, a big lie, or just any lie that hurts you? What really offends you—a little illicit sex, a vulgar profusion of illicit sex, or only that illicit sex which produces illegitimate children? What will call you to responsible civic action— political corruption of any kind, bad politics which makes bad laws, or any political evil which causes a friend an injustice? To which will you say, "Enough of this" and do something about it—one elderly hungry person, the hunger and malnutrition of a nation, or one pitifully hungry child with a bloated belly? How much thievery is tolerable—street crimes, corporate crimes, or any crime that robs our households?

Do you see the significance of the questions? I urge you to determine the identity of the proverbial straw that breaks the camel's back so that you can determine the nature of your response to that next-to-the-last straw on your back. You ought to know both at what temperature you are flammable and what causes such a temperature to rise within you. For some people the determining factor in active indignation is the effect of the situation on their pocketbooks; for others, the consequences of evil for their bodies; for others, the influence of a bad phenomenon on their families; and for still others, the results of a problem in the lives of those whom they love. What is determinative for you, formative in your behavior?

Implied here is the suggestion that anger can be healthy. Recently I read a book on the Psalms written by Daniel Berrigan. I found myself disturbed. Berrigan is preoccupied with the evils of nuclear war. He sees that issue related to every Psalm and comments on it in almost every statement. I had chosen to read the book for meditational purposes. So, I resented the author massaging my soul with barbed wire. But then I became angry about the right things—some of which are identical with the sources of Berrigan's anger. Berrigan has some helpful words, "Anger is a fire in the mind, it gives light to go by, heat, energy."[2] Anger can be "the warmth, the quality, the preserving element of our passion for justice, of our love for others."[3] Such comments remind one of Luther who said, "When I am

---

[2]Daniel Berrigan, *Uncommon Prayer. A Book of Psalms* (New York: The Seabury Press, 1978) 35.
[3]Ibid.

angry, I preach well and pray better.''[4] He could have added ''and act more effectively.''

For many years I have felt that Dylan Thomas's words to his father who was dying have a larger profound moral relevance for all who are really living: ''Do not go gentle into that good night, . . . Rage, rage against the dying of the light.''[5] Much around us should spawn a healthy rage within us. Are you capable of it? Do you have a capacity for rage? Remember that the opposite of love is not hatred but apathy. What bothers you?

Well, there is the question in both positive and negative forms. What, if anything, bothers you? Please do not think that I have an answer for you. The purpose of this sermon is not to provide an answer *for* you but to be sure the question demands an answer *from* you.

An answer is crucial. The difference between knowing is the difference between developing a capacity for loving devotion and caring indignation and an inability for either. In that case, devoid of the capacity for love and anger, joy and indignation, one can meet the Christ and fail ever to serve him, or watch the crucifixion of Christ and offer not a mumbling word of protest. Then, tragically, life takes place only at the level of trivia. One lives minimally grasping here and there for meaning, celebrating the unimportant and seeking to take a stand by way of a Don Quixote-like fighting of windmills. So you see, the question is a crucial one. But, for God's sake and for the sake of others, even more important are the answers which you give to that question.

What, if anything, bothers you?

---

[4]Franklin M. Segler, *Your Emotions and Your Faith* (Nashville: Broadman Press, 1970) 67.

[5]Dylan Thomas, ''Do Not Go Gentle into That Good Night,'' *The Collected Poems of Dylan Thomas* (New York: New Directions Publishing Corporation, 1957) 128.

Friend!

Matthew 26:47-50; 2 Corinthians 5:19-20 (TEV)

Friend! To speak the word or to hear it spoken spawns images.

My four-year-old son was sitting on the back steps of an unfamiliar house to which his family recently had moved from another city. When asked by his mother what he was doing, John Paul explained, "I'm going to sit here until I make a new friend." Friend.

A Los Angeles newspaper ad promoting an agency promising promptly upon request to provide a friend—to send out a friend to sit and talk, to hold the hand of a person hurting or dying, a friend for as long as the caller could pay.[1] Friend.

A freshman boy feverishly seeking to groom himself appropriately and to dress stylishly, regardless of the cost involved, thinking that appearance—the right figures on his shirt, the popular cut for his jacket, the "in" look of his jeans—will guarantee acceptance, associates, friends. Friends.

A female transfer student behaving contrary to her basic personality, cutting corners on integrity, and even compromising her morality seeking so desperately to find favor, to be asked to run with some crowd, to gain entry into a collegiate society. Friend.

A middle-aged adult speaking foolishly and acting abnormally trying so hard to relate to acquaintances in a younger generation. Friend.

A woman in her early fifties seeking a new life and fresh relations rushing to throw off an image of passivity, studying vigorously to master the so-called art of self-assertiveness activities. Friend.

A teenager risking mental and physical health, making every conceivable effort to impress his peers, to be asked to join a group. Friend. Images.

Interestingly, the most striking image of all comes from Holy Scripture. Judas Iscariot, accompanied by legal officials and men of the militia,

---

[1]Leo Buscaglia, *Loving Each Other. The Challenge of Human Relationships* (Thorofare NJ: Slack Incorporated, 1984) 20.

approaches Jesus in the Garden of Gethsemane. As a result of a question-able kiss, captor and captive, traitor and betrayed, come face to face. What on earth was Judas doing? Jesus looks Judas squarely in his eyes and says to him, "Friend" (Matthew 26:50)—Friend!—either "Friend, be quick about it!" (TEV) or "Friend, why are you here?" (RSV) Either way, Jesus calls Judas "friend."

Most commentators judge Jesus' mode of address to be virtually meaningless. Thus, friend was a throwaway term, just a thoughtless way of speaking to a colleague, a word devoid of any real significance. How-ever, some students of the text take Jesus' word to be a term of rebuke, a powerful put down, a greeting dripping with satire. Personally, I do not happen to agree with either of these interpretations. I believe Jesus was se-rious, meant what he said, spoke from his heart when he addressed Judas as "friend." In fact, precisely within this rather strange context and against the backdrop of that astounding declaration, the nature of friendship can be explored beneficially.

In relation to friendship, as at so many other points, culture really has done a number on us. Our cautious, calculating minds have sought to quantify a qualitative concern. A passion for success causes people to count friends like possessions—"Just listen to this list of my friends"; to see friends in terms of power—"I have friends in high places, you know." Making friends has become analogous to collecting trophies. Clarity is needed.

Acquaintances, even close associates, sometimes husbands and wives, are not necessarily friends. Togetherness is by no means synonymous with friendliness. Some of the loneliest people whom I know are among the busiest people, people most in demand, in social situations. Acquain-tances are around them constantly. However, inside they are suffering hor-ribly from loneliness. Tea parties and cocktail hours rarely provide opportunities for nurturing friends. Incidentally, most church fellowship periods are little different in that regard.

Often clubs, fraternities, sororities, and organizations of other kinds are viewed as a form of insurance against friendlessness. Unfortunately, such thought is seriously flawed. Friendship involves far more than a com-mon cause, a shared oath, the same enemy, or even a legal contract. Fra-ternity brothers, sorority sisters, team players, and church members may not be friends. Relating to friends does not require joining anything.

Actually, even our terminology is problematic. Commonly people comment about *making* friends or *having* friends. Most crucial is *being* a friend. Realistically, friendships are found more than formed, discovered rather than designed. It all starts within us.

To talk or to write of a strategy on how to win friends is as ridiculous as to promise a method of not growing older or to commend a diet by which people can eat all they want of anything and still lose weight. None of it is possible! We can develop devoted acquaintances, strategize to assure loyal customers, achieve victories in the realm of new business relationships, but we cannot win friends.

Any authentic interest in friendship must arise within each of us as individuals. The reality of an actual friend is directly related to our personal capacity to be a friend. Consider carefully what is involved.

Friendship is a mystery

A friend is an unexplainable gift of grace. Frequently, friendship catches us off guard. Often only after it is experienced happily is friendship even recognized rationally. Two lives come together as if prepared for each other since a moment in some distant past, but neither individual is aware either of that moment of beginning or of looking for the other person. Both are surprised by joy.

Do not try to explain it or to make sense of it. Like any other mystery, friendship defies such assaults by reason. Strategies to achieve it stop short of it. Clubs to promote it promise more than they can deliver. Setting out to gain it ends in disappointment. Friendship is a mystery to be encountered and celebrated.

Friendship is risky

Vulnerability is a necessity among friends. No safe way to intimacy exists. As Eugene Kennedy has said, "Love's only true measure is our lack of defense in the presence of the loved."[2]

Admittedly, that is a tough realization for most of us. Typically, we do not like disarmament individually any more than we aspire to it nationally. Over against tendencies to play life close to the chest, to hedge our bets, not to say all that we know, and to cover our flanks, friendship de-

---

[2]Eugene Kennedy, *On Being a Friend* (New York: Continuum, 1982) 49.

mands that we open up, expose ourselves, and care with abandon. Sure, we can continue to protect ourselves, to remain aloof if we choose. But, we never will know friendship from such a posture.

Study the risk involved. More hurt is possible among friends than in any other place. Great psychological harm can result from the hurt engendered by friends. After all, no one betrays enemies, only friends. Of course, also among friends are more joy, fulfillment, and meaning than can be known elsewhere. Risk is involved. But without risk, one knows no friends.

Friendship involves visibility

Whoever says that love is blind reveals a radical misunderstanding of love. Love sees very well. Friendships occur only among imperfect persons. True friends are fully aware of each other's weaknesses as well as strengths, faults as well as accomplishments—but neither matters. Each person is loved for who he or she is—good and bad together.

As a friendship develops, visibility is enhanced. Often a person in a newly discovered loving relationship will say, "I see things as I have never seen them before." "The world looks different to me now." True. Joy becomes more desirable than pleasure. Sexuality is more significant than being sexy. Personhood overshadows personality.

Friendship requires liberty

Friends are unavailable on demand, unmakable by force. Friendship is a gift freely extended from one person to another. No deals are struck, no bargains argued, no contracts written—"I will be your friend if you will make this change." "Become like I want you to be and I will be for you." No. Friends accept each other, let each other be.

To be perfectly honest, though, some liberty is sacrificed once friendship is experienced. The friend takes precedence over most everything else. Flexibility and spontaneity become full associates of liberty. One never can tell about a schedule exactly. A friend may need to talk, to take a walk, to get a Coke, to look at a rainbow, or to play just at a time when we had other plans. Oh, well!

Friendship is costly

In a sense, friendship is unnatural. Our tendency is to want to make gains, to accumulate resources for ourselves. By way of contrast, befriending is a form of dying. Self-giving is essential in being a friend. Kennedy's words are helpful once again: "The truest path to friendship lies in the effort to make our best selves available to others, to strip ourselves of the obscuring loss of selfishness, and to give more than we demand."[3] Only as we forget ourselves are we likely to find a friend. Never is the intention involved one of gain— acquiring friends in order to gain popularity, developing friends in order to use them professionally. Just the opposite.

Friendship develops when two people discover a relationship that is more important than self-will, more valuable than life itself. Each friend dies a little individually in order to live more fully for the other. A recognition of how much must be lost provokes appreciation for how much the relationship really means.

Friendship offers security

Allow me quickly to point out that the security of a friendship is a different kind of security from that commonly known—a security related to ultimates; a security unaffected by membership dues, graduation exercises, and geographical separations. A sense of total well-being exists because of the relationship with a friend. As long as each friend lets go of himself or herself, the other friend will never be lost. Only friendship can provide such confidence.

Troubles will not topple a true friendship. After all, friends know no greater meaning than that to be found in bearing one another's burdens. Distance and time, weaknesses and wants are no obstacles, only opportunities for growth. Within intimacy, even death is robbed of its power to intimidate. As one has said, "Blessed are those unafraid to be friends, for they are also unafraid to die."[4] Some dying has already taken place in order to make possible a friend. The true source of living has been tapped.

Alright. So, that is what is involved. What about the work of friendship? Work is the wrong word, actually. No how-to-do-its are involved.

---

[3]Ibid., 150.
[4]Ibid., 32.

The dominant requirement in a friendship is to be a friend—enjoy it. We even can be irreverent *with* our friends, but never irreverent *about* our friends. Friends laugh together and cry together, share both victories and defeats. Friends talk with each other about anything and everything or nothing. They chatter about trivia and pour over profundity. Friends can be themselves with each other.

Oh, sometimes we must learn to wait. Not everyone's internal clock operates on the same time. One friend may get to a place, an emotion, an experience, a desire, a conclusion, before the other one arrives. Just wait, though. Waiting is part of the work of a friend. Eventually the two will share it.

Friend. Now look at the word again. Friend. Consider it once more on the lips of Jesus as he addressed Judas. Do you see? Do you understand? Jesus had resolved to be Judas' friend. Not even an outright betrayal on the part of Judas could alter the realization of that intention in Jesus. All of the right components were there— liberty, risk, cost, mystery, and the like. When Jesus said, "Friend," he meant it. Let us learn from it.

Such is the nature of true friendship. It begins within each of us and reaches out in selfless love—not to gain anything, but to give everything. Amid so many disposable devotions, superficial relationships, cheap, throwaway associations, and store-bought, do-it-yourself approaches to human relations, God gives us the potential to live as friends. Friendship is a divine gift to the world. But more. God offers Jesus as the model— one who is our friend and whose sole purpose in life is to relate to us in love so that we can be the friends of God. Think of that—the friends of God. Friend. Grace.

To be friends with each other is to know the joy of compassion. To be friends with God is to experience redemption.

Friend. Friend to you. Friend with God. Let it be, O God. Let it be, dearest Friend.

Can You See?

Mark 8:22-26

Did you ever notice how utterly disinterested Jesus was in adjectives attached to persons? Of course, in some instances a gospel writer incorporated an adjective in a story—a rich man, a sick child, a poor woman. But in every instance, Jesus saw only a person—not a rich, sick, or poor person, just a person. Nouns— persons—were what mattered to him.

Adjectives related to people are blunting human sensitivity and destroying the possibility of community. Modifiers of persons are mitigating against relationships between persons. Let me explain.

Anytime we focus on the adjectives that describe persons and allow the modifiers to dominate our attention, we run the risk of losing sight of the persons. Jesus can help us. In fact, that is at least a part of the promise of this brief passage in Mark.

For a long time, I read the account of Jesus' encounter with the blind man at Bethsaida as just another healing story. But, recently, I saw something different here. Notice when the restoration of vision was complete. This is not only a story about healing but a comment on what it means really to be seeing. Here is a criterion by which to measure sight, a principle by which to determine when a person really can see.

True sight involves the capacity to see people as people! The man in the story could see some things—people who looked like trees walking around. Jesus made it clear that at that point the man was not yet healed. People are not things and should not be seen as things. Almost worse than living with total blindness, no sight, is functioning with only half vision— sight that lumps people together as things, thus robbing persons of individuality—and believing that such insufficient sight is complete.

True vision is essential for functioning with sensitivity and working for community. Only with full sight can we penetrate that which modifies persons and accurately perceive persons themselves, disregard adjectives and focus on nouns.

To say we have a problem in this regard is to make an understatement of extreme proportions. We are merchants of modifiers, seeing descriptions of persons rather than persons and peddling as the whole truth the errors of our partial vision. By way of adjectives, we determine the worth or worthlessness, meaning or nonmeaning of persons. In fact, eventually labels replace the individuals to which they are attached so that personhood comes to be understood as, for example, young, middle-aged, or old. Each description carries a load of common assumptions: young persons are restless, energetic, and ambitious; middle-aged persons are tense, overworked, and crisis prone; older people are passive, undependable, and dying. Little wonder that some people of a young age dress as if years older while persons of advanced years attempt to wear the clothes of the young. Both tendencies bear witness to our culture's fascination with adjectives—appearances, descriptions, rather than persons.

Let us consider the Lord's question intended to evaluate vision. "Can you see anything?" (Mark 8:23 TEV) What do you see—suave people, sloppy people, handsome boys, beautiful girls, ugly men, drab women? Are you half-blind? Do people appear to you as rich or poor; good or bad; married, single, or divorced; smart or uneducated? Does your vision penetrate adjectives and really comprehend persons? When you look at a group of people, do all of those involved get thrown together? Do you see trees walking, adjectives describing, or what? "Can you see anything?"

Both the question and its answer are terribly important. Apart from clear sight, dangerous attitudes and actions can ensue. *Stereotyping* can occur. All black-skinned people look, think, and act alike just as do all people with yellow skin tones and those whose skin is white. All rich people are insensitive, boisterous, and obnoxious. All old people are forgetful, unreliable, and over-the-hill. All poor people are lazy, uneducated, and shiftless. Can you see? Persons are robbed of their individuality and thrown together in a distorted unity. Sometimes even legislation is enacted to enforce the stereotypes of our inadequate vision. Can you see?

Unfortunately, only a short, quick step separates stereotyping people from *manipulating* people. Assembly-line workers must be made to function like machines. That simply is the system and we must have production. Administrators are institutionally oriented bureaucrats who should be attacked regularly in service of their humility and tricked or cheated when possible in the interest of equality. Employees are the property of corporations and can be moved about like checkers with little or no regard for personal interests. First-year university students passionately seeking acceptance in a group are easily controlled victims of older and wiser collegians who use them in an indeterminable number of ways. Can you see?

Do I have to tell you the end of this pitiful process? Stereotyping people and manipulating people result in *depersonalizing* people. Finally, individuals disappear and only categories remain. Danger abounds. The "competition" must be defeated at all costs. "Opposition" must be eradicated. "Enemies" must be silenced. Lest we ever lose sight of the human potential for depersonalization and the extreme horror of such a situation, we have for our perusal pictures of the smoke-filled skies over the furnaces of Auschwitz and Dachau. The fuel for those fires consisted of the individual bodies of people lumped together into a category—a race that was to be eliminated.

Jesus would have none of this. He saw persons as persons and called on others to do the same. A *demon-possessed* man had been chained and relegated to a burial place by his society. Jesus saw a man—a man—beset by the demonic, and set him free. A mob gathered to stone an evil woman. Jesus saw a woman—a woman—who had done wrong and offered forgiveness. A *boil-infested* man had been condemned to life apart from his family. Jesus saw a man—a man—who had contracted leprosy, and healed him. Do you see the almost total disregard for adjectives in Jesus?

Adjectives allow us to categorize each other, to utilize each other, to destroy each other. We are not as trees walking or as any other *thing* for that matter. We must be able to see each other as persons.

Frederick Buechner began his participation in the prestigious series of Lyman Beecher Lectures by recalling the very first lecturer in this program. In 1874 Henry Ward Beecher rose to speak to his Yale audience after only a brief period of preparation, an almost sleepless night, and a nervous morning in which he cut himself shaving. Back at his home rumors were rampant about Beecher's involvement in a questionable relationship with a woman and indications were that a crisis was at hand. Buechner wanted listeners to know the humanity of the lecturers.[1] Such a start helped listeners to hear a man, a *man,* not a lecturing man or a preacher man, just a man.

A friend of mine acted heroically during one of the critical stages of the civil rights struggle in the 1950s. In fact, NBC News called his bravery a turning point in the whole movement. Many years after that event, the two of us talked together about it. My friend told me how frightened he

---

[1]Frederick Buechner, *Telling the Truth. The Gospel as Tragedy, Comedy, and Fairy Tale* (New York: Harper & Row, Publishers, 1977) 1-2.

was on that occasion. Quite frankly, I was surprised. I had always imagined an idyllic courage stemming from a concentrated commitment. Sure,
my friend had helped some families of another race, but that was not all
that was on his mind that morning. Not all was well in his family or even
in himself.

Can you see? Can you see human beings? We must never lose sight of
the personhood of the people around us. Martin Buber's observation is
profound. We would do well to heed its implications.

> Every person born into this world represents something new, something that
> never existed before, something original and unique. It is the duty of every
> person . . . to know . . . that there has never been anyone like him in the world,
> for if there has been someone like him, there would have been no need for
> him to be in the world.[2]

Such an understanding of individuals—an intolerance for labels, adjectives, pigeonholing descriptions—contributes to our own concept of self-
identity, to our capacity for compassion and ministry and to our commitment to community.

Concept of Self-Identity

When we fail to look beyond descriptive titles or labels and see persons, we develop unhealthy views even of ourselves. Everyone seems to
be above us or beneath us, richer or poorer than we are, more moral or less
moral, smarter or dumber. Nervously, we begin to feel out of place. Does
no one else ever feel like I do, think like I think?

That blessed little woman in Calcutta espouses the proper perspective
on how to view others as well as ourselves. Mother Teresa sees even the
beggar in the ditch as Jesus incognito. Thus she tells those who want to
join her in ministry, "If you don't want to smile at Jesus, then pack up and
go home."[3] Jesus incognito! The image of God! Such is the manner in
which we are to see others—and ourselves.

In his unforgettable autobiography, Howard Thurman tells of revisit-
ing his birthplace in Daytona Beach, Florida in order to acquaint his young

---

[2]Martin Buber, *Hasidism and Modern Man* (New York: Horizon Press, 1958)
cited in Edward V. Stein, *Beyond Guilt* (Philadelphia: Fortress Press, 1972) 38.

[3]Mother Teresa, *Words to Love by* . . . (Notre Dame IN: Ave Maria Press,
1983) 8.

daughters with the playgrounds of his youth. All was going well until the little girls spotted a set of swings on which they wanted to play. Thurman froze inside, but outwardly, calmly told them they could not swing there. He promised to explain why later. I read his comments with amazement. Nowhere are his genius and Christian commitment more apparent. Thurman did not label those who had created racist laws by speaking of them with vitriolic adjectives. Rather, he told his children how important they were. Listen to his words, "Never forget, the estimate of your own importance and self-worth can be judged by how many weapons and how much power people are willing to use to control you and keep you in the place they have assigned to you. Your presence can threaten the entire state of Florida."[4]

Can you see? All people are important. If you know that, then you know that so are we. Both the heroes and the scoundrels or our society have their own hurts, anxieties, dreams, and disappointments like we do. Realization of that truth enhances our

Capacity for Compassion and Ministry.

No one particularly likes to love a group or to serve a conglomerate. Yet, if we can see individuals—untarnished by labels, good or bad—we can relate personally, helpfully, lovingly. Not surprisingly, most of history's greatest atrocities have resulted from throwing people together as faceless, unidentifiable parts of a mass. Soldiers can destroy a city under the guise of military bravery, but who wants to kill a group of first-grade school children, a young college graduate beginning his first job, or an excited young lady pregnant with her first child? Such are the activities involved in destroying a city.

Somewhere I discovered and subsequently became intrigued by Roger Fisher's thought and suggestion about the action of any United States president who orders the beginning of a nuclear war. Fisher fears the president making such a crucial decision surrounded only by well-scrubbed military personnel and set apart totally in some sterilized, isolated crisis room. There the president is psychologically removed from those people who will be the victims of his decision. Thus, Fisher has proposed that the codes nec-

---

[4]Howard Thurman, *With Head and Heart* (New York: Harcourt Brace Jovanovich, 1978) 97.

essary to unleash a nuclear attack be implanted next to the heart of some volunteer who will always accompany the president. Then, if the president ever decides to launch our nuclear weapons, he first will have to take a knife and plunge it into the chest of one of his aides in order to retrieve the proper instructions for beginning the battle. Personally, he will have to be responsible for the bloody death of one individual before he kills thousands more by pushing a button or making a phone call. Here is an attempt to see through generalized adjectives and focus on the specifics of individuals.

Surely when we see people as people, our anger is tempered and our prejudice weakened so that we are moved to compassionate ministry. Here is the way to exercise our

Commitment to Community.

As long as adjectives dominate interpersonal relationships, we will have cliques and mobs, street gangs and business clubs, mafias and other conglomerates of unrelated units, but not communities. Community becomes a possibility only when we see and major on how much we have in common rather than on what separates us.

Community is possible—here and now. However, the realization of it demands some alterations in our perspectives. We must see persons. Keep in mind that the professor who lectures so confidently and brilliantly in the classroom well may be radically insecure in his office and home. The student whom we greet with a casual "How's it going?" simply nods rather than relate the pain of a recent letter in which she learned of the death of a close friend. Think of that possibility. You meet a counselor who seeks to give help to others while desperately needing help for himself, perhaps from you. A secretary has trouble typing a project because she is still reeling from a fight with her husband before arriving at work. A dorm mate is traumatized by destructive doubts. Can you see?

We live not amid a conglomerate of competing entities but within a potential fellowship of cooperating, caring persons who can share together joys and sorrows, hopes and disappointments, failures and plans. To that kind of community—a fellowship without labels—we can be committed. The makings of it are all around us. Just look.

Can you see? What do you see here and there—an administrative type, a professional sort, a fraternity officer, an independent leader, a sorority sister, an athletic achiever, a scholarly student? No. No. No. Look again. Ask for Jesus' help with vision. Allow him to touch your eyes. He has given sight before. He will do it once more. Now, what do you see? People. Yes, people—persons like you and me with all kinds of potential for communion.

Keep on looking in such a manner and surely you will begin relating. No, they are not trees—that is the sight of half-vision. You do see persons, individuals created in the image of God. Yes, that is the sight of real vision. Such sight can make all of the difference in the world— even in an institution, even in you, and in me.

Thanks be to God for the gift of his Son Jesus Christ who helps us not only to overcome blindness but really, really, to see! Amen.

Angel, Did You See Me Smile?

Genesis 18:1-8; Hebrews 13:1-2

Whoever wrote "The Letter to the Hebrews" provided us with interesting, even intriguing advice. The essence of the author's counsel was "Christians, keep on loving one another. Don't neglect to welcome guests. This is how some without knowing it had angels as their guests."

What? Angels? After a check of the Greek text as well as numerous reliable translations of it, I must tell you that the essential thrust of this passage is the same in all versions—angels incognito; an entertainment of angels without an awareness of angels. We can receive angels without realizing that our guests are angels!

Historically, these biblical words have been interpreted in relation to the socioreligious context within which they first appeared. Many itinerant ministers—preachers, missionaries, and the like—traversed the Graeco-Roman world. Though it is unlikely that any of them had taken a vow of poverty specifically, many of them undoubtedly were poor. Customarily, when these traveling ministers entered a city, they sought out brothers and sisters in the faith for a place to rest and for food to eat. Thus, a standard admonition within the Christian community was for people to open their homes for the entertainment of such guests. But, the heavenly tag gets all of the attention related to this rather ordinary activity—some of the guests could be angels.

Angels? The basic meaning of the New Testament word translated "angel" is a messenger from God, one sent by God. Obviously, various shades of meaning are assigned to the word because multiple descriptions of angels are presented in the Bible. Nowhere in Scripture, however, is there any suggestion that angels must be mystically cloaked, heavily winged figures. Any messenger sent from God properly could be designated as an angel. Appropriately, then, the writer of Hebrews well could have been calling for hospitality to be extended to strangers because of the possibility that some of these strangers could be messengers from God—angels.

Surely, some such interpretation as this enjoyed acceptance in the primitive church. But, are there not broader implications here which in-

...volve a truth that spans the time between the initial appearance of this passage and the present? I think so. Called into question immediately is the place in our lives devoted to hospitality, friendliness, encouragement, and other forms of supportiveness.

Two responses dominate my reflections personally. On the one hand, I am reminded of the gratitude which I feel for those persons who have been hospitable, friendly, and supportive to me. Secondly, I am encouraged to resolve that I will live similarly in a helpful manner in relation to other people. That for which I am thankful is that about which I am hopeful.

Some time back, I retraced some very familiar paths in Louisville, Kentucky. Having spent eleven years in that city as a student, a teacher, and then a pastor, I knew well the regular routes as well as the shortcuts through and to its various communities. While driving down one main thoroughfare in the suburban city of St. Matthews, a very strange thing happened. At one particular point on that street, without any conscious awareness of my actions, my head suddenly turned to the left and my eyes scanned the sidewalk for someone—someone who was not there. Then, it all came back to me in a rush. Throughout my earlier stay in Louisville, almost every time I passed that specific spot, I had seen a certain semiretarded newspaper salesman. Every day—rain, heat, snow, whatever—he was there, usually with a smile on his face and almost invariably with a wave for passersby. I do not know the man's name to this day. He never knew that his attitude and friendliness ministered to me. However, even after several years, I missed his wave!

Do you know such familiar persons of encouragement? Another nameless man who cheered me regularly guarded a busy intersection and helped elementary school children through it in a residential community of Fort Worth, Texas. This man did not have to know people to be friendly to them. A smile crossed his face as he waved his hand in the air anytime anyone passed. Even after our youngest son graduated from the school in that particular community and I no longer had to travel that route each morning, I continued to drive through that intersection occasionally just to see my unknown friend and to enjoy his wave of a hand.

Surely, from time to time, lonely people passed by both of those men and felt cheered by their attentiveness. Each one would wave to anyone as if he had known the person for life. Of course, some cynics could argue that the men acted so cheerfully in the interest of self-gratification. My hope is that each did feel fulfilled personally because of his efforts. Neither one possibly could have gained as much joy as he deserved. Both offered a fantastic ministry of encouragement to those who passed their ways.

Thoughts of other individuals—ministers of encouragement! Angels?—enter my mind. One particular friend in another city seems to make phone calls at just the right times and allow me to get a glimpse of grace. An older lady in a former pastorate physically touched me each Sunday morning with a pat on the arm as we passed each other on the way to our places of worship leadership. Her accompanying words strengthened me—"I am praying for you this morning." or "God bless you as you preach."

Can you name those kinds of people in your life? They are always there when you need them. A letter from one of them or a phone call or a smile or a word timely spoken meets your needs, makes your day. Maybe it is no more than a look across a room, but it is a loving look. These are important persons who should be thanked as well as remembered. Such supportive individuals treat us like angels. Oh, to be sure, we know better about ourselves. A little embarrassment accompanies our thoughts of an angelic identity. Yet, some people relate to us in that manner. Thanks be to God for such sensitive, generous souls.

In expressing gratitude to God for the encouragers in my life, I find myself aspiring to be an encourager in other people's lives; hoping to be for someone else what various uplifters of the spirit have been for me. That realization raises a question or two—where in my life (and in yours) are genuine hospitality and compassionate friendliness so prevalent that people will look for them there? If sometime I do not show up at a particular place and for some reason I fail even to smile much less to wave, will anyone miss my encouragement immediately and eventually take a second look for my wave? At what place in the routine of our days do people automatically expect to see us wave or to hear us say, "God bless you" or just feel our supportive presence? Where is it—at home, in the dorm, at the office, in the student center, on the street?

The importance of such a predictable presence of encouragement is indescribable. A sensitive smile can enhance self-worth even in the life of an individual who is shy by silently communicating, "I see you and I care. You are important." Recognition of another person by a wave of the hand can help lift a shroud of loneliness. In fact, far more is involved than individual reactions to our efforts. Such simple gestures on our part are significant contributors to the building of community. And, who knows, we may have been hospitable to an angel!

In Claus Westermann's book, *God's Angels Need No Wings,* two characteristics of angels emerge from a thorough study of the biblical literature related to these creatures.[1] First, angels invariably show up in common moments amid ordinary activities—arriving at Abraham's tent as three visitors seeking hospitality in the noonday heat, coming to Gideon while he threshed grain, appearing before Joshua as he made plans for battle, singing before shepherds as they watched their sheep, standing before a depressed woman in the privacy of her quarters. If we look for angels only in religious settings adorned by holy garb, we will miss them.

Second, usually angels are recognized as angels in retrospect. At the moment of their occurrence, encounters with angels appear like engagements with strangers, beggars, colleagues, common friends, and persons in need. Only after a response is made to such persons is their angelic identity understood.

On one occasion I heard Wayne Oates reminisce about a lady in New York City who regularly sat at the entrance to Union Theological Seminary. Obviously, the woman did not belong to that institution as a student, faculty member, or administrator. But, she was there by the gateway every day. Finally, someone asked her why she came there so regularly. The woman explained, "Because the people who come by here smile at me."

What would a person see or say who sits where we walk? Why is it that many folks can walk right past each other and never even speak, much less smile? Good grief! What if we have been bypassing angels?

I am genuinely thankful for persons— both well known and nameless—who have reached out to me caringly. They took a chance that I was an angel. I trust that they were not too disappointed when they discovered my real identity. Thankfully, they did keep waving anyway.

I am sincerely hopeful that I can reach out to others similarly in a supportive manner. Oh, if I just knew that a person was Jesus incognito—remember that he said he would come to us unrecognized—or that a stranger was an unidentified angel, there would be no problem. Certainly, I would smile, wave, and probably even jump up and down with greetings. Not knowing for sure, however, I must confess that I fear failure at some point. Really, I aspire to be like those folks who never have to fear missing anybody—visitors, holy or unholy—because they wave at everybody. Never

---

[1]Claus Westermann, *God's Angels Need No Wings,* trans. David L. Scheidt (Philadelphia: Fortress Press, 1979) 82, 92.

do they have anxieties about failing to be friendly or supportive when a messenger from God passes. These people treat everyone like a messenger from God.

"Christians, keep on loving one another," the scriptures say. "Don't neglect to welcome guests. This is how some without knowing it had angels as their guests." Angels!

What if I did not know it was Jesus on the street corner and I showed no sign of friendliness or hospitality? What if I never even looked up from my work and an angel passed me by? No. No, I do not want that. Neither do you want that, I am sure. It must be different. Jesus, did you see us wave? Angel, did you see me smile?

You'll Get Yours

What do you want out of life, really? Forgive me if you are discomforted a bit by my raising this rather heavy question when you may be seeking only quiet relaxation, restive meditation, and perhaps a measure of inspiration. In self-defense, let me assure you that my question is a good one—not nearly so philosophical in nature as many would have us believe, but actually very practical. Where you are today in your feelings, values, studies, vocations, and interests is shaped considerably by your individual responses to that fundamental inquiry. What do you want out of life?

Answering the question about what we want in living—honestly responding to that inquiry, probing to grip the answer we would give in the confidentiality of our own consciences and affirm in the privacy of our own souls, replying without concern for the judgments of family members and the opinions of friends, establishing what we really want—enables us to get in touch with what we are doing—priorities we are setting, agendas we are establishing, sacrifices we are considering, risks we are taking, the future we are anticipating. Whether or not it is in line with the original purpose behind your attention to this sermon, I want to encourage you to grapple with this issue seriously, tirelessly if necessary, because your response not only gives form to the present but shape to the future.

Very likely you will get what you want. Thus, what you seek helps to determine whether or not the content of your future is good news or bad news.

At stake here is a scriptural principle with an application far more comprehensive than is suggested by the specifics of the actual situation out of which it arose. Jesus was talking about worship. His remarks focused on the three most revered disciplines in Jewish piety—prayer, fasting, and alms giving. Speaking about persons who viewed their involvement in these charitable practices as impressive public performances, Jesus raised a question about motivation. Why do people pray, fast, and give alms? Undoubtedly, all of the people present were well aware of religious exhibitionists—those who paraded piety for applause; prayed, fasted, and helped the poor for praise from their peers.

Notice carefully the comments from Jesus. A crucial principle emerges. Three times—in verses 2, 5, and 16—Jesus said that these people—the ones seeking recognition for their dramatized devotion—will get what they want. At first glance, Jesus' words may suggest an assurance of success for such folks. Look again, though.

Jesus was addressing people whose sole purpose in demonstrations that looked like devotion was to gain recognition and praise from others. They prayed, fasted, and gave alms in order to be commended. Jesus said simply that they would get what they wanted—recognition, applause, social commendation. They will get just that. But, no more. Those responses constitute the totality of what they will receive.

Interestingly, Jesus employed two different words for "reward" and thus made his point emphatically. In the first instance, Jesus used a technical, business term, a word from the vocabulary of commerce. When a debt was paid, the receipt given in response was marked "paid in full." That is the meaning of reward as Jesus used it first. In the second instance, Jesus employed a word for reward that meant "render." Significantly he immediately related this term to the work of God. Here "reward" designated a divine response to human action.

Look carefully now at the text and its important principle. Those who desire human praise can get it. Even religious acts can be drafted into the service of a selfish, ego-elevating pursuit. However, the very moment that human recognition is achieved, the whole matter is concluded. Doors to the future are closed. No more joy can be expected. The people have achieved what they wanted.

By way of contrast, those persons who give themselves to the same practices but for a different reason—as obedience to God, in service to God, as worship to God—will have a different reward. For them, the future is open. Possibilities for experiencing joy are unrestricted. Unconcerned about immediate recognition from the human community, these people are put in touch with the kind of meaning in life which is of the highest possible quality. Their reward can be as great, as boundless, as the resourcefulness of God.

Do you see the essential principle of the text and its broad implications? You'll get yours. You'll get what you want. That is the truth which emerges from this passage. Negatively stated, no one can invest in life at one level and expect to derive benefits from life at a different level. Positively put, the quality of life we experience will be determined by the quality of life we pursue.

Please understand that far more is involved here than just a neat cultural cliché or an interesting piece of folklore. All of us have heard the colloquial expression "You'll get out of something what you put into it." Be aware that the scriptural word in this text bears a far more profound significance than that—it is more severe in its warning and more hopeful in its promise.

Recently, I read the results of an annual survey of dominant attitudes among first-year college students. Responses were gathered from 180,000 freshmen in 345 institutions located all across the nation. Prompted by value-oriented questions as to why they are in college and what they want from life, an overwhelming majority of the students surveyed agreed on two priorities. At the top of the list of student values was the individual desire to become an authority in one's field of interest. Second was a commitment to make more money.

Attach to this well-documented fact regarding student interests the biblical principle just enunciated—they'll get what they want, you'll get yours. Remember Jesus' comment to the effect that practices oriented to public recognition will meet with success. Then, ask what is lost—socially, spiritually, and personally. Shudders down the spine are appropriate. If expertise and wealth are the dominant goals in life, then life can be defined solely by intellects and economics, skills and possessions. And, that being said, the issue is ended.

Received as rewards by people who want no more than vocational success and material accumulation are receipts marked "paid in full." But, of course, that is not enough.

What happens to life when fundamental expectations for it do not transcend success in professional skills and an impressive collection of material goods? What is to be the fate of matters of the heart, concerns that cannot be subjected to an analysis based upon cost-effectiveness? What happens to those endeavors that are not popular but are right? Eugene Kennedy observed that "A dried-out actuary calculating cost-benefit ratios would probably conclude that friendship is not an efficient enterprise."[1] So, what becomes of friends? Are personal relationships to be judged impractical?

---

[1]Eugene Kennedy, *On Being a Friend* (New York: Continuum, 1982) 97.

Drawing from her extensive studies related to death, Elisabeth Kubler-Ross has observed that dying patients remember most the simple things in life. When death becomes an immediate reality and life takes on a new sense of ultimacy, people forget business accomplishments and successes in fashion. Most important then are recollections of sharing moments with the person most loved, enjoying a meal with friends, seeing a rainbow, running across a meadow, exulting in a gentle breeze. Romanticism? Just try to tell them that.

If "making it" in the professional societies, scaling the heights of administrative ladders in multinational corporations, and becoming a line item in the annual listing of Fortune's top 500 are the dominant goals in life, then must we not give up such frivolous pursuits as being quiet, praying for divine guidance, and preserving times for worship? How is it with us? Are we so much into success and business and the business of success that no time exists for nurturing the human spirit, celebrating redemptive faith, and worshiping Almighty God?

What do we want? How alike or how different are we when compared with those college freshmen in the survey? Are professional preeminence and economic wealth the summits to which we look? Can we forego meaningful relations with people and celebrations of festive moments for a calculable accumulation of things and professional recognitions by plastic plaques presented over hotel china filled with cold fried chicken and hard english peas?

Think carefully. Choose wisely. Do not forget that the actions of compassionate devotion cannot be determined by computerized measurements and that many of the best and most important decisions of life defy rational justification. If we ever lose sight of a divinely inspired mentality which looks to the world like foolishness, what will we do for persons who prefer to be with people as teachers rather than to invest their lives in other more materially rewarding enterprises, for missionaries who opt for the propagation of faith in other places over the realization of social ease and accumulation of financial gains, for activists who enthusiastically will take on a problem like hunger even if others judge the endeavor impossible or irrational? You'll get yours. We'll get what we go after. Essentially that is what eternity is all about—ultimately receiving what you want, endlessly living with your priorities.

After a visit to Lambarene, Norman Cousins described a scene that I have read as a parable related to the principle I am commending. If Albert Schweitzer had been guided by the most prevalent standards in society, he never would have been in Lambarene. But, thank God, this man made decisions by different criteria. The genius was there in the wilderness—a long way from the applause which had greeted his concerts and the checks which had supported his medical practice in Europe.

Not a day passed that Schweitzer did not find time to play Bach on the old beat-up piano in the compound. Cousins happened upon one such moment. Read his description of it.

> One night, long after most of the oil lamps had been turned out, I walked down toward the river. It was a sticky night and I couldn't sleep. As I passed the compound near Dr. Schweitzer's quarters, I could hear the rapid piano movement of a Bach toccata.
>
> I approached the doctor's bungalow and stood for perhaps five minutes outside the latticed window, through which I could see his silhouette at the piano in the dimly lit room. His powerful hands were in total control of the composition and he met Bach's demands for complete definition of each note—each with its own weight and value, yet all of them intimately interlaced to create an ordered whole.
>
> I had a stronger sense of listening to a great console than if I had been in the world's largest cathedral. The yearning for an architectured beauty in music; the disciplined artistry and the palpable pouring and catharsis—all these things inside Albert Schweitzer spoke in his playing.
>
> And when he was through he sat with his hands resting lightly on the keys, his great head bent forward as though to catch the lingering echoes. Johann Sebastian Bach had made it possible for him to free himself of the pressures and tensions of the hospital, with its forms to fill out in triplicate. He was restored to the world of creative and orderly splendor that he had always found in music.[2]

Schweitzer got his—in a distant jungle to be sure; not knowing anyone was looking on or listening. Here was expertise, but not for recognition—expertise expended in devotion to God and in service to other people. How can we measure the success of that? Must we deem that kind of man or woman ridiculous? How do you compare the happiness of a Schweitzer out in the wilderness living amid what many would call poverty and the happiness of a man sitting in an office suite looking at a bank account which is full but realizing that his soul is empty?

Every day we make decisions that determine not only the immediate direction of our lives but also our ultimate destinies. Given a choice be-

---

[2]Norman Cousins, *Albert Schweitzer's Mission. Healing and Peace* (New York: W. W. Norton & Company, 1985) 116-17.

tween responding to a truly loving relationship and pressing on through an agenda structured for professional purposes, we make a determination about our character as we arrive at a decision. Confronted by an opportunity to offer help which is costly or to invest in an enterprise known for its profitability, we shape the nature of our spirits as we respond.

Remember the principle about reward. Please do not lose sight of the wise and authoritative words of Jesus. You'll get yours! Then, with this principle from scripture in mind, motivated by priorities of the spirit, movements of love, a will to serve persons, and a devotion to God, get on with life. Indeed, go for it! Go for all of it!

God Desires Our Good

What is it with God? What is God about? Sometimes I struggle in my understanding of God's nature and will because of the harsh realities of human existence.

A friend is near the pinnacle of his professional life when a rare disease suddenly causes his death. A missionary who has devoted all of his days to serving God and proclaiming his message of love is left inactive after a freak accident. Two vibrant lives in our midst have been quickly snuffed out in recent days.

What is it with God? What is God about? What does God want from us and for us?

I remember very well one of the first times such questions as these bombarded my mind and challenged my faith. I was visiting with an older pastor when he received word about the drowning deaths of two early childhood twins. He invited me to accompany him as he talked with the grief-stricken parents. In an effort to comfort the two severely troubled adults, my friend explained that though we do not always understand God's ways we have to accept such incidents as the drownings as part of God's will. Everything within me exploded. I felt a rage of resentment. I knew that I did not know how to articulate accurately my convictions but that I did not believe for one minute those drownings were God's will. My faith did not reside in a child killer. Besides, had not Jesus said, "It is not the will of my Father who is in heaven that one of these little ones should perish" (Matthew 18:14)?

Unfortunately, that was not the last time some well-meaning person with nothing else to say displayed a kind of false piety which, when really pondered, created anger—anger towards God. Does God desire the kind of world in which disease triumphs over good intentions, tragedy stops short the accomplishment of noble objectives, and persons die young? What does God want for us?

A preoccupation with such questions has led me to an examination of the scriptures. Look at what answers can be found there. Consider

God's Intention in Creation

From beginning to end, the story of creation is an account of God's plentiful provisions for the good of his people. Man and woman were formed in the image of God and filled with the capacity for a relationship with each other that could produce fulfillment, joy, and even love. Human beings were set down in a world of beauty surrounded by sky and water, plants and animals, which could bring them pleasure. A rhythm for life was established whereby persons could know the meaning of both rest and work. When God assessed the whole situation, he declared it to be "good."

As you well know, right away human beings abused their freedom and exercised their wills against God rather than for God. Of course, God's intention in creation was frustrated. His ultimate purpose was not realized. But God did not give up on his creation. Immediately God acted to restore the primacy of good.

The divine commandments recorded in scripture stand as God's guidelines for a good life. In no sense is this legislation to be viewed as a negation of life. Rather than restrictions on life, the commandments are merciful instructions for life. Law has its source in love. Prohibitions are best seen as statements of grace.

Behind every divine "no" is God's intention for a "yes." We are admonished not to kill, not to steal, not to commit adultery, not to lie in order that we can know a life characterized by dignity and integrity. Divine negatives should not be accepted as divine attempts to deprive people of anything. Rather, the prohibitions are offered in order that people can know the good in everything. Listen to God's reasoning about his people as recorded in Deuteronomy 5:29, "If only they would always honor me and obey all my commands, so that everything would go well with them and their descendants forever." Do you understand? God desires our good. God wants the very best in life for us.

In addition to considering God's intention in creation, look at

God's Purpose in Redemption

Jesus stated clearly God's purpose in redemption. It coincides precisely with the reason for the Incarnation and the nature of Jesus' mission. Look at the Lord's words, "I have come in order that you might have life—life in all its fullness" (John 10:10). How could the truth be made any clearer—God desires good for all of us? Paul stated the same matter in a different manner, "God . . . wants everyone to be saved and to come to know the truth" (1 Timothy 2:4).

Think about it. Our best qualities in life are redeemed responses to God's nature and action regarding life. For example, we love because God has loved us. We hope because of what God has placed in our hearts. Just look at what God wants us to experience. Paul called the whole package the "fruit of the Spirit"—"love, joy, peace, patience, kindness, goodness, faithfulness, gentleness, self-control" (Galatians 5:22-23). That is what God desires for us. Who can question the divine will for human good?

Based upon God's intention in creation and purpose in redemption, I must conclude that God desires good for us. More specifically, I believe God wills life and health, food and freedom, enjoyment and salvation for every person. God is our friend, not our enemy. God desires our good.

"But that is not the whole story," you say. "Tragedies still occur. Injuries alter life's plans. Deaths come all too soon. Problems prevent the realization of righteous purposes." How are we to view such difficulties? How are we to cope with the dark side of life?

The apostle Paul struggled with these very kinds of thoughts as he contemplated God's sovereign goodness. This is the way he reasoned it out for believers: "We know that in everything God works for good with those who love him, who are called according to his purpose" (Romans 8:28).

What the apostle did not say is every bit as important as what he did say. Paul did not say that everything is good. Evil is an undeniable reality. Tragedy is a fact of life. A part of the price of living in an open universe as free-thinking people is coping with the results of bad decisions, dastardly mistakes, and deadly diseases. In fact, complete immunity from such negatives would cost us nothing less than our very humanity. But, that is not the last word on the subject.

Evil remains evil. Tragedy exists as tragedy. But, neither tragedy nor evil, nor anything else, can ultimately defeat us. Paul explained why. God works even in the dark side of life to bring some good from it. This does not mean that God causes the evil or sends the tragedy in order to accomplish good. The truth is simply that God deals with the givens and does not stop working for good despite the presence of problems and difficulties.

Nowhere is God's power in the face of tragedy more clearly demonstrated than in the crucifixion of Christ. By any standard of measurement, the crucifixion of Christ represented the ultimate cosmic tragedy. As Joseph McCabe has commented, "The death of Christ is the best reason in the world for being an atheist.''[1] Amid the darkness of that distant Friday afternoon nobody had any reason for any confidence that God desires our good. But, wait. Consider the totality of the event. God acted in the midst of the world's most despicable evil to accomplish his greatest good. The cross of Christ, a symbol for death, became the ultimate way to life.

In reality, today as back then, we often find God most present in that very experience which seems most to deny his goodness. Calamities come. But God continues to desire and to work for what is good for us.

Some people have confessed that because of the presence of God in their lives, the best has grown out of the worst. Alexander Solzhenitsyn wrote, ''And it was only when I lay there on rotting prison straw that I sensed within myself the first stirrings of good. . . . I say without hesitation: 'Bless you, prison, for having been in my life' ''[2] Hear Malcolm Muggeridge, ''The only thing that's taught one anything is suffering, not success, not happiness, not anything like that. The only thing that really teaches one what life's about—the joy of understanding, the joy of coming in contact with what it really signifies—is suffering.''[3]

Does all of this mean that God desires suffering for us? Absolutely not. The truth at stake here is that of God's ability to work even in the negatives of life to bring about something positive. Remember Paul's words, ''We know that in everything God works for good with those who love him, who are called according to his purpose'' (Romans 8:28).

So, what are we to conclude? What do we do with tragedy? What is it with God? What is God about? Here are my conclusions.

First, God is our friend, not our enemy. Thomas Merton recalled that while the Germans were desecrating a church somewhere in Poland, a German sergeant, wild with excitement, stood in front of the altar and challenged God. The man yelled to the heavens that if there was a God surely he would want to prove his existence by striking down such a bold,

---

[1]Joseph E. McCabe, *Handel's Messiah. A Devotional Commentary* (Philadelphia: The Westminster Press, 1978) 72.

[2]Alexander Solzhenitsyn, *The Guleg Archipelago 1918–1956. An Experiment in Literary Investigation,* vol. 2, trans. Thomas P. Whitney (New York: Harper & Row, 1975) 615, cited in Malcolm Muggeridge, *The End of Christendom* (Grand Rapids MI: William B. Eerdmans Publishing Company, 1980) 47.

[3]Malcolm Muggeridge, *Vintage Muggeridge. Religion and Society,* ed. Geoffrey Barlow (Grand Rapids, Michigan: William B. Eerdmans Publishing Company, 1985) 115.

important, terrifying fellow as himself. Nothing happened. God did not strike him down. The sergeant departed, still excited and probably the unhappiest man in the world. God did not act like a Nazi.[4] God's justice is vastly different from that of human tribunals. God is for us as a friend, not against us as an enemy.

Second, tragedies will continue to occur; but we are not alone in them and need not be defeated by them. As long as we remain persons, not puppets, mistakes will be made, evil choices will bring tragic consequences, potentially life-defeating events will take place. However, God does not desert us in bad times. We are not left alone. God is with us. In fact, God well may be most present at the very moment he seems most absent. As one wise man observed, when God does not rule, he can overrule. God works even amid evil to accomplish good.

Finally, God desires our good. I know it from creation and redemption. I find it in personal experience. God is pro-life in the nonpolitical sense of that important phrase. God desires the best in life for us.

The point of the sermon is well made poetically by Katharina von Schlegel in words that were set to music. Hear them with profit and conviction.

> Be still, my soul: the Lord is on thy side;
> Bear patiently the cross of grief or pain;
> Leave to thy God to order and provide;
> In every change He faithful will remain.
>
> Be still, my soul: thy best, thy heavenly Friend,
> Thro' thorny ways leads to a joyful end.[5]

---

[4]Henri J. M. Nouwen, *Thomas Merton: Contemplative Critic* (San Francisco: Harper & Row, Publishers, 1981) 91.

[5]James W. Cox, *Surprised by God* (Nashville: Broadman Press, 1979) 38.

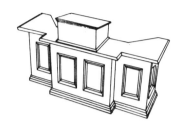

Christian Year

The Shadow of Christmas (An Advent Sermon)
The Gospel of the Wise Men (An Epiphany Sermon)
He Cried (A Lenten Sermon)
He Died (A Good Friday Sermon)
We Laughed (An Easter Sermon)
Saints Step Forward (An All Saints' Day Sermon)
A Reformation Spirit (A Reformation Day Sermon)

The Shadow of Christmas

Isaiah 9:2, 6-7; John 1:1-5, 10-14

At first I wanted to argue with the imagery. Helmut Thielicke, a noted German theologian and preacher, called Christmas "now only a shadow for us."[1] A shadow? Surely he had mixed his metaphors and perpetrated an improper image—I thought. Christmas is a festival of light. Burning candles in our windows and blinking lights on our trees serve as reminders of the light that came into the world, the light that shined in the darkness, the light that darkness could not best, the light that enlightens every person, the light of the world. Why a shadow? What is the source of the shadow? Can Christmas legitimately be considered a shadow now?

Could it be that Christmas in our world actually is more of a shadow than a light? Maybe the answer to that question should be treated chronologically and geographically. It is a long, long distance to Bethlehem in more ways than one. Perhaps we are now so far away from the Christmas event that evidence of its light reaches us only in the shadow that it throws across the years. We celebrate Christmas more as an old tradition than as a fresh start on creation. Our world has little time for lowing cattle, kneeling shepherds, and camel-weary wise men or wise women. And angels, angels are an anachronism. We are pretty far removed from the light.

Maybe the answer to our question about Christmas as a shadow requires us to delve into a little philosophy—Platonic philosophy actually. Could it be that now Christmas is a shadow because we celebrate not the real but only an image (a shadow) of reality? Observe our behavior. Listen to our talk. Christmas is a parenthesis in the year, a bracketed good, a culturally recognized "time out." For a week or so, or at least a day or two, we focus on human fellowship and goodwill. Everyone is right-intentioned. Peace is lauded and love is praised almost to a point of nausea. But no one is kidding anyone else. All know that on December 26 old agendas

---

[1]Helmut Thielicke, *Being a Christian When the Chips Are Down,* trans. H. George Anderson (Philadelphia: Fortress Press, 1981) 103.

will return as Christmas trees are taken down. People quickly get back to reality—the stock market, defense systems, political negotiations, arbitration about justice—the "real" stuff of life. The shadow has been duly noted and celebrated, but the event of Christmas—the real event of Christmas—has been missed.

Maybe Thielicke is right. Perhaps today Christmas really is only a shadow for us. If so, or if there is even an outside chance that such is the case, we must ask what can be done about it. How can we get at Christmas reality once more? Now is the time to focus on that concern. Thus, let's take a long look at the situation.

We do have to deal with this matter of *distance*. Distance separates us from the Christmas reality—which appears to us either as a dim light in a far-off past that casts a long shadow into the present (the shadow is far more noticeable than the light that causes it) or a faint light at the end of some futurist tunnel (we walk in the shadow in pursuit of a light that seems elusive at best, if not unreachable at worst). Thus, it appears to us that Christmas celebrations never are what they used to be or what they could be. The reality seems far removed from the here and now.

Jesus came so long ago and so very far away. Now the nature of much of our talk about him brings to mind Mother Goose rhymes, not biblical texts. Many persons cannot distinguish between reality and fantasy, historical facts and cultural myths.

From today to that yesterday—the evening of the Savior's birth—is a great, great distance. The world was different then. Those people who gathered to see the newborn child did not look like we look. Incredibly, they were not into stocks and bonds so much as into sheep and goats. Needs were different in many ways, though quite possibly more like ours than we dare to think. Loyalties were in conflict then just as they are today, though the objects of human affections were characteristic of the age.

Looking back to the Christ event causes us to acknowledge how much water has run under the proverbial bridge since then—indeed, so much water with such great turbulence that the bridge almost has been swept away at times. We have fought massive, bloody wars. We have built and destroyed one kingdom after another. A nomadic way of life gave way to an agrarian economy which in turn gave way to industrialization. Sounds from around the manger were muffled by the rat-a-tat-tat of assembly line machines and the boom of an atomic bomb. Then came secularization—a god which denies the importance, or even the existence, of any gods.

How far have we come? Hear secularized Madison Avenue at its worst in the text of this printed advertisement: "Don't you have more to celebrate than Christmas? Give her a diamond."[2] When we need an alternative for Christmas, when Christmas is merely an occasion for some greater purpose—Christmas is only a shadow. We are cut off from the reality to be celebrated.

Things need not be this way. Indeed, things must not be this way! Distance is no difficulty for the divine. The very message of the season is that God can come to us. The "hound of heaven" sniffs us out and tracks us down the corridors of time. Wherever we are, God finds us and comes to us. Christ is born today, in this century, here where we live.

We also have a problem with *depth*—the depth of our loneliness, the depth of our despair. For many, the matter is not one of doubting that God can come to us but one of believing that God does not come to us. We are too lost, too guilty, too messed-up, too depressed for God to bother with us. Surely, He must go on to bigger and better things, appear to people who have got it all together, not risk any tarnish on His holiness by mixing it up with us and our sinfulness.

Our culture has done a bad number on us. Efforts have been made to reshape even the shadow of Christmas. How does Christmas come to us—in Nieman-Marcus glitter, through a blue-light special at K-Mart, in the purchase of a startling surprise, through the arrangement of an unforgettable trip? Society has spoken loudly enough to drown out scriptural truths. Thus, people are left to reason: no money, no Christmas; no beauty, no holiday season; no cheery smiles, no Advent greetings; no parties, no nativity. In our four-color, slick-paper Christmas catalogues we have perpetrated a lie—that Christmas is only for beautiful people, the in-crowd with money. Certainly, many folks conclude, Christ would avoid the depths of our existence.

Don't you believe it, regardless of how many times you hear it! If we must have everything in order for Christ to come, there is no glory in his coming. If we must be perfect to assure Christ's arrival, there is little need for divine grace and power. If we must be smiling and confident for Christ to appear, then the gospel is a joke. If Christ does not come to the depths of our existence, he really does not come at all. Here is the danger of celebrating the shadow rather than the reality of Christmas.

---

[2]"Campbell's Notebook," 3/1:4.

Look carefully at the light—the first light, that primeval light, which came into focus at Bethlehem. God was coming into chaos. Jesus was born amid turmoil. People were griping about taxation. An insecure king was getting ready for fighting and killing. Just look at the people who first welcomed Jesus into the world. None of them could make any invitation list for holiday parties then or now. They were outcasts, poor folks, and despised shepherds for the most part—people for whom the depths of life were home.

No depth, not even despair, prevents Christ's coming. Rather, more than once desperation has been the cradle in which the divine presence was discovered.

Paul Tillich related an unforgettable incident in which a child was born in a grave. During World War II some people in Wilna, Poland lived in a grave in a Jewish cemetery for a while. Only there could they hide and hope to escape the Nazi gas chambers. While there, assisted by an eighty-year-old grave digger, a woman gave birth to a child. When the baby first cried, the old man prayed aloud, "Great God, hast Thou finally sent the Messiah to us? For who else than the Messiah Himself can be born in a grave?"[3] Well, that child was not the Messiah, but an important point about the Messiah had been made. Christ comes to us in the depths—at our worst times, in our weakest moments. Christ is born.

Please, please let me pull you out of or push you away from the shadow of Christmas and introduce you to the reality. Neither distances nor depths separate us from Christ, prohibit his coming to us. The birth of Jesus Christ is real and ready to be celebrated.

John Killinger wrote of a dear friend who had hit upon bad times. Because of a variety of unfortunate circumstances the man was denied tenure in a large university. After a lengthy period of agonizing while searching for a new position, he landed a job with a seminary consortium. However, only a few months later the consortium folded. The man fell into a deep depression. Trying desperately to find help, he discovered an ancient method of praying practiced by St. Ignatius and his monks. He tried it.

Fantasizing about a relaxing scene, the man sought complete relaxation before God in order to be completely open to God. He imagined a warm, sunny day on the beach. While walking and enjoying the fresh air,

---

[3]Paul Tillich, *The Shaking of the Foundations* (New York: Charles Scribner's Sons, 1948) 165.

he saw a bottle floating in the tide and he could see that a message was rolled up inside it. He knew the message was for him. The man dashed to the edge of the water and then waded through the surf until he rescued the bobbing bottle and opened the little scroll it contained. Tingling with excitement, he began to read, believing that this must be a word from God for him. What he read was a Latin phrase "Hodie Christus natus est." His spirits suddenly plummeted. The man had expected some important message, information about a job, suggestions on how to help his family, divine guidance for a way through this troublesome time. Before him was only a Latin phrase which he had known since childhood. "Today, Christ is born."

Initially very disappointed, the man kept on praying. The familiar phrase kept returning. Finally, he saw the truth. "Today, Christ is born." Then, it happened inside of him. The indwelling Christ was with him. He was not alone. Fear and anxiety receded. A quiet confidence was experienced. The man began to live from the center again—from the center where Christ lived in him.[4]

Please hear the good news. Come out of the shadow. Neither distance nor depth need stop you. Today, Christ is born. He can live in you. You can live from the center with him. That is the Christmas reality, the light which shines even in darkness. Don't miss it. Don't miss him. Whatever you do this year, don't miss the Christmas reality, the divine light. Today, Christ is born!

---

[4]John Killinger, *Prayer: The Act of Being with God* (Waco TX: Word Books, 1981) 78-79.

The Gospel of the Wise Men

Matthew 2:1-12

Christmas is over. Or is it? Of course, the special day has passed. Undoubtedly by now festive decorations have been boxed for their eleven-month period of storage. Carols are quiet. Classes have begun again. But, the shining light of Bethlehem, the star of the incarnation, has not been extinguished. In fact, now—after the celebration of Christmas Day, at the point of our embarkation on a new year, now—is the time to focus upon a segment of the Christmas narrative that has invaluable long-term implications for our lives. Church liturgists refer to this season as Epiphany.

Some folks—the wise men specifically—came late to the Christmas scene. I realize that no one would ever know that from the looks of our Christmas greeting cards and other pieces of seasonal art. Popular portrayals of the first Christmas have three wise men traversing the streets of Bethlehem or kneeling before the manger of Jesus. I have heard various individuals vigorously defend the authenticity of such depictions. They remind me of the woman who was upset because her neighbor's Santa Claus had only four tiny reindeer. In disgust, she declared, "Well, if people don't read their Bibles, what can you do?"

Actually the Scriptures are silent on the number of visitors who came from the East to visit the Christ child. Only tradition, based on the number of gifts mentioned in Matthew 2, specifies three. Unknown as well is the specific time at which these people arrived at Jesus' side. Some evidence suggests that as much as a year or two had passed between the event of Jesus' birth and the moment the wise men entered his home and laid their presents at his feet.

Despite an absence of numerous specific details, the story of the wise men is fraught with significant meaning. Here were no fly-by-night, faddish religious enthusiasts. These people had committed themselves to a long and trying journey and persistently pressed on it until they found the Savior. They were venturers, visionaries, dreamers, willing to follow a star. We need their kind.

Ponder with me three important implications drawn from the gospel narrative about the wise men. Each one has profound meaning for us. First,

The gospel is a call to adventure

In truth, if faith is found at all, it is found on a journey. Recall the Old Testament model par excellence— Abraham. Faith was discovered as faith was exercised. Abraham could not sit in Ur of the Chaldees and stockpile enough faith, accumulate enough assurances, to guarantee him success on his journey into the desert. Abraham found faith as he ventured forth in faith.

Similarly, the wise men of the gospel narratives discovered Christ only after they had departed from the security of their homes and the familiarity of their studies and ventured forth toward Christ. Think about it. They set out on a journey with no known destination, embarked on a pilgrimage with no defined end. Had they not done so, think what they would have missed. Strength for the journey came on the journey. Guidance from the star developed as they followed the star. At the end of it all they stood before the Savior of the world.

Faith does not come to those who play life close to the vest, to people who sit back and refuse to move until all questions are answered, every direction is received, and strength for the journey is assured. Arriving at Christ's side necessitates launching out onto an open-ended pilgrimage. No one can discover faith apart from an adventure into faith.

How many times I have heard someone reflect on the past: ''I never would have thought that I could have endured such suffering'' or ''In the face of death, I found a peace that I could not possibly have anticipated.'' I understand. The economy of faith is such that faith is always experienced on pilgrimage, supplied as needed, offered as required. The more one ventures, the more one discovers. As a matter of fact, you never will feel you have enough faith for anything in advance. If you wait to act until there is no venture, then there is no faith. By biblical definition, faith is launching out with a certainty about things unseen.

I like Samuel Miller's words: ''A man of faith is bound to be a man on his way, a viator, the eternal 'sojourner on earth,' who has here below 'no abiding city.' He knows not; he believes. He has not; he hopes for. He sees not; he obeys. And his road is not defined like the unvarying orbit of a star, but is permanently venture; it is created under the feet of those who take it.''[1] Change the masculine pronouns to feminine and the truth is the same.

What good news for us as we stand on the front edge of a new year. We need not be tentative, hesitant, or afraid. We do not have to put life on hold until we feel that we have enough faith successfully to negotiate every situation. We can begin to journey now—journey with the assurance that with every trying situation will come the faith necessary to cope with it. Indeed, to stand back and wait for faith will be to miss it. We will know faith as we begin walking in faith.

Just as the road to Christ involved adventure for the wise men, so does the way of Christ invite adventure for us. The gospel is a call to adventure.

Look again at the narrative of the wise men. Another important truth is apparent. Consider the significance of the

Knowledge that goes beyond reason

Call it intuition, imagination, a hunch, wonder, or even faith. I refer to that resource that allowed, or maybe impelled, the wise men to follow a star. It is the same phenomenon as that which permits us to pursue dreams, to risk love, to venture by faith.

I am reminded of the line of Eleazor Hull, a great sea captain of the last century. Captain Hull sailed more remote seas, brought home greater quantities of oil, and lost fewer crewmen than any of his excellent peers. All of this was the more remarkable because Captain Hull had no formal navigational training of any kind. When asked how he guided his ship so infallibly, Hull explained, "Well, I go up on deck, listen to the wind in the riggin', get the drift of the sea, and take a long look at the stars. Then I set my course."

One day modernization caught up with the good captain. The insurance company that covered the vessels of Captain Hull's employers decreed that it no longer would write policies for ships whose masters did not meet formal standards of education in the science of navigation. Fearful of the new rule's application to Captain Hull, executives of the shipping company presented their case to him. Surprisingly, the old fellow responded positively, indicating that he had always wanted to know something about

---

[1]Sermon by Samuel Miller, Harvard Divinity School, cited in Carlyle Marney, *Priests to Each Other* (Valley Forge PA: Judson Press 1975) 71.

science and saying that he was willing to study it. Arrangements were made. Captain Hull attended school and graduated near the top of his class. When he returned to his ship, he set out on a voyage that lasted for two years.

Upon Captain Hull's return, a delegation met him at the docks. They wanted to know how it was to navigate by the book. "It was wonderful," Captain Hull explained, "When I wanted to know my position, I'd go to my cabin, get out all the charts, work through the proper equations, and set a course with mathematical precision. Then I'd go up on the deck, get the drift of the sea, listen to the wind in the riggin', and take a long look at the stars. And correct my computations for error."[2]

To be sure, you need to learn all that you can learn in the classroom. Intellect is important. Education in the proper utilization of reason is invaluable. But remember, never forget that there is more. A full life requires the ability to discern the rumblings of the heart, to be sensitive to the sweep of the spirit, to know when calculations, measurements, and carefully reasoned judgments are inadequate, to realize the importance of pursuing a dream, to understand the necessity of following a star.

To depend upon the dictates of reason alone is to miss some of life's most wondrous gifts. Always, always, there are "good" reasons not to venture, "sound" arguments not to risk, "accurate" calculations to sanctify the status quo. What if one never moved beyond reason? The wise men would not have met Christ. Captain Hull would have steered his ship off course. And, what will happen to you?

In all fairness, I should warn you that to live as I suggest may cause criticism. Almost certainly such knowledge beyond reasoning evokes scoffing. Though indispensable to the betterment of life, star followers are often indicted as kooks. Devotees of the indefinable are derided as ignorant. Really wise people are castigated as fools. But, just think what this world would be like did we not know such fools. We need them. In fact, God calls them and the gospel shapes them.

Now one thing more— a final truth implicit in this biblical text. Christ—the baby in the manger who is destined to become the Savior of the cross—

---

[2]William Muehl, *All the Damned Angels* (Philadelphia: Pilgrim Press, 1972) 16.

Christ is for all people

Do not miss a subtlety of this passage that is wrapped up in the identity of the travelers. By Jewish standards, the wise men were pagans— individuals who stood outside of holy history. Thus, their acknowledgment of Jesus' birth was inestimably significant. From the very beginning Jesus is depicted as a person for all nations. No one sect can lay claim to Jesus alone. Jesus is for the world.

Obviously, here is an impulse to missions—a motivation as well as a rationale for missionary activity. The one we meet in Bethlehem is the one we are to make known to the world. To discover Christ is to desire to share Christ. Every Christmas is to be followed by an Epiphany. What God has made known to us we are to introduce to others. The good news of Jesus is to be spread before all people. Think of the ramifications of this truth for our presence in this place. Obviously, here is an impulse to missions.

More subtly, here as well is a word of encouragement. Christ is for all people—that means all kinds of people. No one will be turned away from him. He will accept what any one of us has to offer. Think about that. Christ is ready to receive the irreligious as well as the religious, the stranger as well as the familiar, the defeated as well as the victorious, the depressed as well as the elated. The path to Christ is open to all of us—to the epitome of sinners as well as to the model saint. We can make our way to Christ if we have not been sitting piously in the temple pondering his presence or responding to singing angels who appeared amid our work. Folks like us are welcome. Our worship is acceptable. Jesus is for all people.

At the very beginning of this new year, we will do well not to put Christmas away too quickly. Let us turn again to the Christ child and read once more the narratives of his birth. Focus particularly upon the wise men. Learn from their experience. Celebrate Epiphany. Embark upon the adventure of faith. Give priority to that knowledge that goes beyond reason. Acknowledge your accessibility to Christ and your acceptability in his presence. Capture the conviction that he is for all kinds of people. Rejoice in the realization that Jesus is the Savior of the world.

He Cried

Sometimes I get tired of trying to be strong. Do you? Culture really has done a number on most of us. Building a facade of strength and confidence or maintaining such a structure of subterfuge, regardless of the energy involved, somehow seems to be a more worthwhile endeavor than honestly confessing hurt and reaching out for help. Our society seems to place its highest premium on personalities who exist like robots—mechanical entities devoid of feelings, programmed to keep on running without distraction in every situation. Well, maybe an electrified conglomerate of metal gadgets can encounter problems and do no more than beep once or twice before moving on. But not a human being—at least not this human being.

Criticism hurts. Betrayal gnaws at one's innards and threatens to break one's heart. Disappointments prompt despair. Shattered dreams show up as nightmares. Why must we deny this reality, act as if sadness doesn't matter, forever shrug our shoulders in the midst of disorienting problems and mutter, "I'm alright," labor to assure that people always will say, "Look how well adjusted he is" or "my what great stamina you possess"? Why?

Jesus cried. That is a statement straight out of the authoritative Word of God. Jesus cried. *Jesus*—the Son of God, the Son of Man, the Savior of the World, King of Kings, and Lord of Lords—cried. Jesus *cried*—allowed warm tears to fill his eyes, permitted those tears to stream down his face, enabled persons around him to hear his sobs and to witness other symptoms of his sadness. Jesus cried.

Not surprisingly, some folks are very uncomfortable with this particular insight about Jesus. In fact, a few people have tried to twist it piously, to explain it so that the weeping was not really weeping. Not all Gnostics are dead. Some commentators drone on and on about the theological significance of Jesus crying.

To be sure, the act was not without theological significance. Here, as elsewhere, Jesus revealed the nature of God, the nature of a human being, and the nature of the church—his body in the world. God is compassionate. Divine love is not devoid of hurt. God is interested in the valleys as well as the peaks of people's lives. To be human is to know sadness as well as joy, to cry as well as laugh. A true community, a fellowship of God's people, is sensitive to weaknesses and sorrows as well as to strengths and happiness. The church is a place for crying as well as singing.

When Jesus cried, truth was revealed. Granted. But that is not primary. Jesus' tears were not carefully calculated, premeditated means of teaching a lesson. Jesus did not weep pedagogically. Jesus cried because he hurt. All kinds of factors figured into the situation. Jesus was tired, disappointed, and sad. Then came the proverbial "one more thing," "the last straw." He cried.

Standing before the tomb of Lazarus, Jesus realized that he had lost a good friend. Additionally, other good friends told him that if he had only been with them Lazarus would not now be dead. What a load! Jesus cried. Looking out over Jerusalem from his vantage point on the Mount of Olives, Jesus realized that his ministry was near an end and that this so-called Holy City was racked by economic corruption, political tyranny, religious hypocrisy, and physical violence. How sad. He cried.

Why avoid it? Why try to explain it away? Why be embarrassed by it? What a burden we place on our children when they come to us with stumped toes or hurt feelings and we say to them, "Be a little man and don't cry" or "Act like mother's big girl and stop crying." A friend in the dorm unintentionally adds pressure rather than relieves it when we are told, "Stop that childish crying and straighten up." Whatever made us think that to be mature means to be emotionally sterile, consistently passive? Jesus cried.

Will Campbell spoke profoundly to this matter in one of his novels. One soldier happens upon another and finds him crying. Immediately an apology is offered. Then the one sobbing begins to relate to the stranger a synopsis of his past, a review of his own personal pilgrimage. Finally, the man who had just come on the scene inquires as to why he is being told all of this. Listen to the explanation. "Because you saw me cry. And when a man sees another man cry, that means he knows all there is about him."[1]

Do we imagine that we appear more in control, less vulnerable, if we do not cry? Does some strange kinship exist between Peter the disciple and

---

[1]Will D. Campbell, *The Glad River* (New York: Holt, Rinehart, and Winston, 1982) 5.

us? Remember, Peter did not want Jesus to wash his feet. He could not bring himself to acknowledge that he needed that. He was above such service. Peter did not even know his own capability for evil. What about us? Do we fear that if we are seen crying we admit our humanity, confess too much sensitivity, reflect immaturity?

Has someone sold us a bill of goods about faith erasing all hurts and wiping away all tears? Jesus cried! Real faith sustains us laughing or crying. We do not have to carry faith or protect faith. Faith carries us and protects us.

Holy Week is a time for honesty. No superficial stuff has any rightful place here. Masks are to be taken off and facades torn down. We cannot be worshipful if we cannot be truthful. Maybe, just maybe, the tears of Jesus can help us in this regard. Perhaps this is a period of time which can be used best by learning to cry—at least inwardly if not outwardly.

Consider please two observations—one about the purpose of crying and the other about its promise.

Crying gives expression to the deepest sentiments of the heart. Crying is a matter of conscience as well as a means of coping with pain. Not to cry is to become less human rather than more human; to deaden life rather than to deepen it.

Tears are often in order. When loving relationships are torn asunder, tears should be present. No hurt is involved only if people do not matter. And if people do not matter, God help us. If people do matter, so what if we let them know it?

Jesus cried over severed relationships—out of compassion. He also cried out of conscience—because of a creation in disarray, a city bent on immorality. Tears are in order when we see people who have sold out to success, witness individuals who have sacrificed integrity for popularity. What about the people in our global village who cannot get to the table—who are dying of starvation or living with malnutrition? Not to cry seems insane. Presently, the governments of this world are spending billions of dollars per day on instruments of war. For only twelve billion dollars per year we could provide every person on earth with adequate food, clothing, education, housing, and health care. How can cries of anger and tears of sadness be held back?

Remembering the events of this week makes me want to cry. When thinking is clear, I know that I could have been a part of the crucifixion crowd. Oh, sure I have faith. Of course, I believe. But, so did they—faith of some kind, belief of some sort. Within all of us is the capacity to seek total control, to take life into our own hands, to attempt to drive out the Son of God.

When we repress our feelings, refuse to reveal our emotions, fight back our tears, what do we do to ourselves and what do we communicate to others? Are people just not that important to us? Are issues not that significant? What kind of people are we if we can take everything in stride? Jesus cried.

Look, though, at when he cried. Before the tomb of Lazarus, crying preceded laughing and rejoicing. On the Mount of Olives, crying preceded resurrection, promise, and celebrating. Actually, for a Christian disciple, the two go together—always.

Show me a person who cannot cry and I will show you a person who cannot laugh. Crying and laughing come from the same place within our souls. If we steel ourselves against weeping, ultimately we so deaden our lives that we become incapable of rejoicing. Those who know the greatest happiness in shouting hallelujahs are those who have known the most profound sadness in the shedding of tears. Crucifixion and resurrection are but two parts of one life. If we are to know the latter, we must know the former. Those best able to celebrate life have known the agony of death. Laughter is rather empty in a person who has never known the pain of sorrow. But one does not negate the other. Both go together in real life.

For Christians, crying is not a permanent condition—acceptable, yes; understandable, yes; normal, yes; but not permanent. Often singing follows the sobbing, shouts of hallelujah come on the heels of cries of despair.

Please be assured that this place, this site of worship, right here, is a place in which you can cry with acceptance as well as celebrate with encouragement. I promise you that. Only as we care enough about each other to allow one another to cry, sometimes to cry for one another, and often to cry with each other over situations which destroy—only then will we be the kind of community which is truly committed to Christ and ready to endure crosses as well as to embrace resurrections.

Of course, at moments I would like to do away with crying altogether and certainly to get rid of all of those situations which cause crying. Yet, I get tired of trying to be strong, attempting to act like all is well when it is not, seeking to try to cover up pain with a smile. The Christ whom I meet in the midst of Holy Week cried. He gives me, and you, permission to be human, to feel pain, and to weep if necessary.

Sure, I wish alternate routes to joy were available. However, there is simply no way around the pain, no way to the resurrection which bypasses the crucifixion, no avenue to forgiveness without repentance, no possibility of repentance without confession. But—hear this—it's alright. It really is.

Jesus made possible the pilgrimage. By his wounds we are healed. By his example we are encouraged. Our passions are caught up in his Passion. He—Jesus—cried.

'He Died

Wouldn't you know it! The Messiah finally comes, we receive him, and he gets killed. That is just our luck. Here we were at last ready to believe in someone, ready to follow him joyfully, ready to be obedient to him totally, and then this dastardly act occurs. I suppose it could have been expected.

To be truthful, most of us were a little disappointed. We kind of thought that faith ought to help us out a bit—you know, make business better, life easier, goals loftier, bank accounts larger. However, he had talked so much about service that we suspected things might not be as we had anticipated. Then he started those commendations about love for enemies, forgiveness for wrongdoers, help for the hurting, gifts to the poor, initiatives for peace instead of acts of retaliation. Not everyone took it as well as some of us have dealt with it. We did not want him killed, but certainly we can understand how it happened and why. It is such a shame.

We want Christianity, but honestly none of us thinks it has to major quite so much on that gory cross. Jesus was a good man to be sure—the Savior. But must we forever focus on his mandate for repentance and his insertion of a cross into his invitation to discipleship? Life is pretty heavy already. More than enough pressures weigh on us presently. For our day, is it not far better just to recall the rejoicing, to emphasize his blessings, and to ponder his good promises? If there must be a Good Friday, and the cross must be presented, let us put roses around it, sand down the splintery rough edges of it, drape it in fine linen, or adorn it with lilies. A cross tastefully done can add to the decor of the place, exist as a thing of beauty rather than as a symbol of trouble. But, not a crude cross please!

Jesus died. Jesus—the Son of God, the Son of Man, the Messiah, King of Kings, and Lord of Lords—died! Jesus died— breathed one last time, closed his eyes, stiffened, grew cold and lifeless. No gospel writer sought to soften the blow. The reality is stated rather matter-of-factly. Jesus died.

Interestingly, the community of faith has never been able to get away from that truth. Every time the story of redemption is told, the crucifixion of Christ is remembered. More is involved than some sick preoccupation with death, a masochistic fascination with failure. From the very beginning, believers have lived with the conviction that this death had unique meaning. So, perceptive pilgrims do not dodge it—only report it and seek to deal with it. Jesus died.

Honestly, I prefer other parts of the gospel to this one. I really like that section about considering the lilies, remembering the birds, and knowing the assurance of God's compassion and provision for us. Beatitudes are a pleasure to ponder. Joy is prodded. Happiness is encouraged. Even some of the harder sayings about love and forgiveness have a special appeal because of their promise, practically speaking. But this matter of Christ's death is different. I prefer to turn my head, to look another way, to turn quickly past the pages about passion and to read again the stories of resurrection. Of course, it cannot be done that way. Though at times the cross does not seem to make sense, without the cross none of it makes sense. I prefer other parts of the gospel, but without the cross the narrative is not even gospel.

Jesus died. I know one reason that bothers me. What killed him then would kill him again, now. Ultimately, he would not have fared any better if his appearance could have been delayed until now and scheduled for here. Prejudice has not ceased. Superficial religion has not subsided. A tendency to look out only for "number one" continues. People still prefer an insipid peace at any cost to conflict for purposes of redemption. Outsiders are still treated as outsiders. Tradition—even a bad one—remains more precious than innovation. What happened then would happen again. I simply do not want to face into that.

Jesus died! I know it bothers us. Please, though, take it seriously. Do not dismiss it too quickly or attempt to bypass it completely. If we will not face Christ's death honestly, we will not live courageously. Besides, there is promise here. Strangely, that which is a stumbling block is also a source of encouragement. The most offensive dimension of the gospel is the same as that which is most special and incredibly beneficial. Look at it.

Despair seems to dominate—at least at first glance. Some kind of cosmic version of "Murphy's Law" appears operative. The best that has ever been among us receives the worst of which we are capable. Hatred is our response to love, violence our reaction to grace. All of the evidence seems to affirm the cynic's philosophy—good guys not only finish last, they get clobbered. Wrong prevails. Justice is nonexistent. Love cannot last long in this world.

As if it were not enough for an innocent man to die because of the guilt of others, Jesus dies with a sense of radical solitude. He who came to be with everyone senses that he has not one—not even God. "My God, my God, why hast thou forsaken me?" (Mark 15:34) New Testament scholars point out that the language contained in the earliest manuscripts of Mark is even more descriptive of Jesus' solitary agony—"Why hast thou given me up to shame?" "Why hast thou cursed me?"

Jesus died. "Where is any promise in all of that?" you ask, "you indicated that some promise was involved." Such a scene well could be an incentive to atheism.

Please do not miss the next comment. Precisely at that moment of overwhelming despair Christ was completely in compliance with God's will. Just as darkness appeared to be winning the day, a tiny spark of light was set to shining. God did his best with our worst. Christ was pinned to those cross ties not only because of human rebellion— sin—but also because of divine compassion—grace. He died. But more, he died according to God's will. He died for us!

Here is not only the promise of our salvation but the promise of divine assistance in times of spiritual depression. Learn from the cross. Jesus felt separation from God. But God was not absent. As George Bernard Shaw reportedly said, "Though we crucified Christ on a stick, he somehow managed to get hold of the right end of it." That was God's doing.

At those times when we flounder around spiritually, doubt more than believe, rebel more than obey, God stays with us. God remains faithful to us even as we struggle over unfaithfulness to him. At least at those moments, we take God seriously. We seek to work out some kind of decision about devotion to him. God matters. Though we may feel completely separated from God at such times, he remains with us. He can do with our worst moments what he did with Jesus'.

Does that mean, then, that we can be done with this crucifixion matter and get on with other things? No. No. Jesus made very clear that acceptance of the call to discipleship meant shouldering a cross of our own every day, continually dying to one way of life in order to live more fully in another.

Jesus died. So must we. But in faith, by God's grace, this death is not the end of everything but the beginning, not ultimate termination but the creation of a future, the first step of salvation, entrance to the journey along which eventually death itself must die.

He died. God, forgive us.
He died. Great God, accept our thanks.

We Laughed

He cried. He died. We laughed!

I know it sounds strange; the sequence is rather weird. Oh, the laughter came neither immediately nor quickly. But ultimately, finally, laughter did come. And, for believers, laughter remains constantly.

How did it happen—then? How could reflections move from crying, dying, and crying about dying to laughing? How did disciples get from muffled sobs about death to unrestrained shouts about life? How did attention shift from the killing place called Golgotha to a laughing place—somewhere, everywhere, in a back room for an evening meal, along the seashore at a fish fry, in the recesses of a believer's soul? How?

Resurrection! One word explains it, the most characteristic word of the New Testament—resurrection. One event clarifies it, the most staggering development in all of creation—resurrection. One experience satisfies the inquisitiveness, the most crucial experience in redemption— resurrection. Resurrection. That is how it happened. He cried. He died. He arose. We laughed.

How does it happen—now? How do *we* get from crying to laughing? How do sighs of sadness become shouts of happiness? How, now? Actually, the same way really—by means of resurrection; faith in resurrection and a resurrection faith.

In the oldest traditions of the church, Easter sermons always began with jokes. You read my words correctly—jokes. Priests and preachers alike heralded the good news laughing. The somber whisper "He is risen" became an ecstatic shout "He lives" and eventually an exultant laugh. He cried. He died. He arose. We gasped. We laughed.

Of course, laughing and crying can be separated only for purposes of emphasis and discussion. Ordinarily the two are intermingled; so integrally intertwined that to tear out either one is to destroy the other. Tragedy and triumph are interwoven in the fabric of a full life and so are our responses to each. Persons of faith know both how to cry and how to laugh.

Admittedly, crying sometimes seems to be most dominant. Laughter appears to be only a diversion from the drabness, if not sadness, of life; a welcomed distraction from the ordinary; a jocular aside from reality. Not so. Not so! In fact, laughing is the final reality. Sorrow is only the penultimate for the person of faith. The author of Revelation stated it symbolically. Many people of faith have affirmed it experientially. Joy is the ultimate. Believers laugh finally.

From the perspective of an Easter faith, look with me at what has transpired to inspire joy and to provoke laughter.

Values Are Reordered

Christ turned traditional morality upside down. Then, when stern-faced legalists tried to set it right again by getting Christ on a cross and out of the way, they failed. They failed magnificently. Values were reordered forever.

Never again could things take precedence over people and that posture be acceptable. Now love was considered more important than law. Compassionate service to people in need was given a place of preeminence over strict obedience to some code or creed. Justice was made less important than grace.

Now, what a person did was viewed as just as important as what a person did not do. Moral goodness was defined with positive content. Acting right became just as significant as not acting wrong. Mandates which involved a blessed happiness took their rightful place alongside prohibitions which required stern discipline.

Individual traitors, swindlers, and even adulterers were accepted alongside the institutional righteous. Hated foreigners were held up as good examples to be followed. Poor people were praised. Rich people were questioned. Movers and shakers in society, first-century pushers, were warned that prominence is not nearly so desirable as service. Winning was associated with losing and dying was viewed as a prerequisite for living.

Perhaps people could have discounted such chaos had Christ quit with the cross. Maybe life would have returned to what many thought was normal. But, it was not to be. The resurrected Lord would not let well enough alone. No human-constructed cross would be allowed to stand as God's final word on this matter. Moral reorientation was for real. Values had been reordered.

People looked and laughed. You can bet that Mary and Peter laughed.
No sooner had Jesus emerged from the tomb than he talked to this woman
whom most folks would have avoided like the plague. If that was not
enough, among the first words spoken by the risen Lord was a statement
of desire that Peter be told of his living presence. Christ remembered with
love the one who had denied him with fear.

Think about it. Consider this resurrection truth and the realities of our
lives. Set them side by side if you dare. What do you think of the pushing
and shoving of status seekers, the clamoring for economic success, the attempt to give life meaning by making it busy, the hunger for recognized
accomplishment? We look and we laugh—somewhat nervously, a little
sarcastically, a whole lot hopefully, and redemptively.

Standing in the light of resurrection faith, look again and see that

Fear Is Abolished

Whatever else the resurrection communicates to us, loudly and clearly
comes the truth that God can take our very worst and bring great good from
it. Easter—God's action— followed Good Friday—human action. Never
forget that fact. Then, in light of such a sequence, think of the confidence
which is inspired and the security which is provided by it. Little wonder
that through the ages believers have laughed.

The worst that people can do to us is as nothing compared with what
God can do! When that truth is grasped fully, fear is abolished and laughter
resounds.

Reflecting on his experience as a prisoner of war in a Nazi compound,
Victor Frankl came to see the art of living in terms of a capacity for laughing. Without laughter, no doubt he and his colleagues in misery would have
died in the presence of their enemies. However, laughter persisted even in
moments of terror. Strikingly, some of the prisoners of war actually laughed
out loud each day as they listened to the announcement of those persons
selected for execution. In that laughter was power. Fear was stripped of its
ability to influence them for evil.[1]

How else do you explain the faithful courage that accompanied believers through those tumultuous years after Christ's ascension? A ragtag

---

[1]Colin Morris, *The Hammer of the Lord. Signs of Hope* (Nashville: Abingdon
Press, 1973) 96.

group of social misfits set out to change the world for the glory of God! Apparently, they had no fear. Why should they? After all, they had seen the worst the world could do to a person and they knew how God had handled it. They laughed. They walked right into danger, sometimes even into death, laughing.

Such was the spirit of Sir Thomas More as he was led to his execution. Because his integrity had been considered a crime, the man had suffered greatly. However, he retained a sense of humor even for that moment of ultimate horror. Tradition has it that as More approached the headsman's ax, he drew his beard aside as he placed his head on the block and said, "My beard, at least, hath done no treason."

Hear this. The promise of the past stands in the present. Resurrection is for us. Thus, assurance continues. "If God is for us, who can be against us?" (Romans 8:31 TEV) We laughed.

Look, again.

Festivity Is Encouraged

Athanasius, a patriarch in the church of antiquity, once stated that "the risen Christ makes life a continual festival, a festival without end."[2] Consistent with that recognition, in many church traditions this period of the year is recognized as a festival time. Easter is considered a feast of joy and freedom.

How really sad it is that so many people have missed completely the life-affirming, joy-provoking significance of Christ's resurrection. This event was God's affirmation of life—an affirmation that invites celebration.

Certain tribes of Latin American Indians continue faithfully to observe the Stations of the Cross without any recognition of the Feast of Easter. As a result, the religion of these people is life negating, happiness defeating, in nature. Rituals of remembrance lead to masochism and self-inflicted lacerations. How tragic! Yet, what should we expect of people who live only at Holy Week? If we knew no more truth than that of Good Friday, how could we ever lift our heads again, much less our hearts? How could we ever stop crying, much less begin laughing?

---

[2]Jürgen Moltmann, *The Church in the Power of the Spirit. A Contribution to Messianic Ecclesiology* (New York: Harper & Row, Publishers, 1975) 109.

For too long too much of the church has preached the victory of Easter but lived like Good Friday was the only reality. Our world is sick for a dearth of healthy festivity. We as the people of God can help. Christ is risen! He lives! History has moved beyond Good Friday. Let the festivity begin. Finally we see the light and invariably we laugh.

Look once more.

Hope Is Celebrated

People without hope cannot laugh. Similarly, people who cannot laugh have no hope. The reality of Christ's resurrection births both laughter and hope.

Somewhere I read how James Angell verbally and experientially commended a celebration of the resurrection-inspired hope. The reality of Christ's resurrection births both laughter and hope. One Easter Eve this Presbyterian minister received word that his daughter had been killed in an automobile accident. On the next day, he preached in pain. (Incidentally, most, if not all, good preaching is intimately acquainted with pain.) His words on that occasion went something like: "Easter is the gift of life because it is the gift of seeing, the power to hope, the will to believe that beyond death is God and life and that our lives are mortgaged to both of these truths."

Not long ago I lost a good friend by death. She died suddenly, prematurely, unexplainably. Recently, her husband and I shared a meal and talked. Never has this man worn his emotions as outer garments. I have always recognized his faith as solid but never as loud. Bill and I talked about Liz's death, his experience of the sufficiency of faith, and then, at his insistence, about hope. Not much time had passed since Liz died. Easily I could have understood it if he had not yet grasped a recognizable hope. With some hesitation, my friend related to me how he felt some people might not understand the feelings that he experienced as he followed the casket out of the church building to the accompaniment of music of praise which concluded the memorial service for his wife. Bill said he found himself wanting to shout for joy—in the midst of grief, wanting to shout for joy; on his way to his wife's grave, wanting to shout for joy. Thank God, Bill has found firsthand the reality of a hope that can be celebrated beside a grave as well as in a nursery. In his own way, Bill smiled. I smiled. Later, we laughed together.

He cried. He died. We laughed.

You know why. Resurrection! Values were reordered. Fear was eliminated. Festivity was encouraged. Hope was celebrated. We laughed.

Please do not misunderstand. I know problems surfaced again. Suffering reemerged with great fury. Believers were persecuted terribly. Some of the very people who laughed because of faith soon died because of faith. The resurrected Christ carried nail prints in his hands and the scar of a wound on his side. I do not commend a laughter of naïveté or irresponsible escape. Rather, I speak of a higher reality, the final reality. Before all was said and done, believers laughed again. They always do. So can we.

My much-missed good friend Grady Nutt said it best. Eleanor, his greatly appreciated wife, passed the comment along to me at a special moment of pain and need. The words are not scripture, but they sound like scripture and square with scripture. ''When the world shakes its fist and says, Good Friday! God comes back with dogwood, redbuds, and jonquils, the crocuses and butterflies of life, and says, Easter! Easter! Easter!''

What can we do but laugh!

Saints Step Forward

1 Peter 2:1-10

In one of his typically fine sermons, Leslie Weatherhead told of a conversation that took place late one evening in a college dorm. A student posed the question, "What do you want to be?" A variety of responses was offered. Some present wanted to achieve academic distinction. A few focused on the winning of athletic prizes. Others desired to fill a professor's chair. One sensitive young man said, "You fellows will laugh at me, but I want to be a saint."

Most likely we too chuckle at such an assertion. We have stereotyped saints. In our minds saints are always persons from a distant past whom we recognize as heroes of the faith. Saints are considered different from everybody else. Sainthood is viewed as a kind of suprahuman category. Saints are thought to be the kind of historical figures that properly belong in stained glass windows. We do not commonly associate the title of saint with any of our contemporaries and certainly not with ourselves. We have stereotyped saints.

We will do well to be instructed by the Bible. According to the New Testament, all of Christ's followers are saints. That includes us. To be more specific, sixty times in the New Testament Christians are called saints. Did you hear the words of Peter as he addressed disciples of Christ? Peter said, "You are a chosen race, a royal priesthood, a holy nation" (1 Peter 2:9)—synonyms for saints. In his Corinthian correspondence Paul referred to all people made new by Christ as "saints" (1 Corinthians 1:2). That means you. Clearly within the pages of the Bible all persons reconciled to God are considered saints.

This sermon is a summons for you to take seriously your identity as a saint and to step forward responsibly. Please be done with the idea that saints are solely characters from the past who lived perfectly. Saints are persons—present as well as past—who take seriously their dedication to God. Saints succeed and fail. Saints laugh and cry. Saints are victorious and make mistakes. Saints are people like us who live out their devotion to God. Would that all of us shared the sentiment of the student in Weatherhead's story—"I want to be a saint."

Sainthood is not an honor bestowed by the church
but a way of life demanded by Jesus Christ

The biblical word used to identify a saint was related to holiness. In fact, the New English Bible translates the plural form of that term as "God's people." The same word used in discussions of the holiness of God is present in statements about this kind of individual. The scriptures indicate that such holiness is derived from devotion to the call of God as sounded in Christ.

Sainthood is not a superior category of discipleship created by the church. In fact, the status of sainthood is not so much attainable by an individual as attributable to God. God makes saints of his people—all of his people.

In Max Beerbohm's story entitled "The Happy Hypocrite" a wicked man named Lord George Hell fell in love with a beautiful, virtuous young lady. In order to woo and win the innocent woman Lord Hell donned the mask of a saint. As the story goes, the trick worked and the two people were married. Years later a cast-off girl friend from Lord Hell's past showed up and sought to expose him for the scoundrel she deemed him to be. This woman dared Lord Hell to take off his mask. Sadly Lord Hell removed the covering and to the amazement of all revealed the face of the saint he had become while wearing the mask of a saint.[1]

Sanctity is the result of God at work in the souls of his people. By way of God's presence and grace, one becomes a saint—a person in whom that work, grace, and presence are realized. A saint is a person who lives in constant communion with Jesus Christ through faith and devotion. As James Earl Massey says, "The saint is a God-claimed person whose life shows that claim."[2] Saints are people whose service in the cause of redemption reveals the transforming power of the risen Christ.

Sainthood is not an honor bestowed by the church but a way of life demanded by Jesus Christ.

Sainthood is not an expression of perfection
but an indication of faithful obedience

Obviously, followers of Christ are not flawless. Read again the personal problems presented within the very New Testament letters addressed to "saints." Paul called the Corinthian Christians "saints" but challenged

---

[1] Frederick Buechner, *Wishful Thinking. A Theological ABC* (New York: Harper & Row, Publishers, 1973) 52.

[2] James Earl Massey, *The Soul Under Siege. Dealing with Temptation* (Grand Rapids MI: Francis Asbury Press, 1987) 76.

them regarding their disunity and immorality. Disciples of Christ are saints not because of perfection but because of forgiveness.

In reality, sainthood is a search for depth—an effort to recover the life-changing nature of New Testament Christianity, to major on what is major in Christianity, to give up anything that is inconsistent with faith, to practice a stewardship shaped by sacrificial service oriented to Christ, to love as he loved, to forgive as he forgave, to minister as he ministered. To be a saint you need not attempt to be someone you cannot be but strive to be who you can be under God. At stake is not the issue of personal ability but the crucial matter of availability to God.

In George Bernard Shaw's play *Saint Joan* a moment comes when Joan of Arc is trying desperately to get Charles, an insipid, spineless man, to show some initiative. Exasperated, she shouts at him that there is one thing he never has learned. Intrigued by her statement, he asks what it is. Joan says, "Charlie, you have never learned that we are put on this earth not to do our business but to do God's."[3]

Sainthood is not an expression of perfection but an indication of faithful obedience.

In 1521 at the Diet of Worms, the cause of Christianity was helped immensely by the actions of a saint. Martin Luther refused to recant on his spoken and published statements regarding the sole sufficiency of faith in Christian salvation. You know his words "Here I stand; *Ich kann nicht anders*—I cannot do otherwise." Luther did not possess unusual courage. Rather he was possessed by the message of the New Testament. Luther was not elevating himself to a position of ecclesiastical supremacy. Rather, he was offering himself in faithful submissiveness to the sovereignty of God. Luther was not perfect in doctrine or ethics. However, the monk from Wittenburg was persistent in seeking to be obedient to God's leadership. Luther was a saint.

As we approach All Saints' Day and Reformation Sunday this year, I want to challenge you to accept your God-given identity and to express it responsibly. You are saints. *You* are saints! Please step forward and live as saints. We must never substitute superficial Christianity for the real thing. We must never settle for less in discipleship than the mission to which Christ called us. You are saints.

---

[3]Herbert O'Driscoll, *A Year of the Lord* (Toronto: Anglican Book Centre, 1986) 133.

Please hear this. Saints step forward. In an age in which pessimism is present and despair is dominant, we need some harbingers of hope. Saints step forward. In a world in which nations get rich off war and settle disputes by violence, we need some vigilant peacemakers—devotees of reconciliation who wage peace. Saints step forward. In an international community in which staggering numbers of persons die daily from malnutrition and starvation, we need some conscientious people who not only pray for daily bread but share it. Saints step forward. In denominations which are torn by strife, we need some apostles of understanding to labor for unity. Saints step forward. In a society in which people are judged ruthlessly and condemned categorically, we need some practitioners of grace who demonstrate love. Saints step forward. In fellowships of religion where people are plagued by guilt, we need some heralds of forgiveness. Saints step forward. In a government in which distrust and deception are all too prevalent, we need some truth tellers. Saints step forward. In relationships in which promises are broken and commitment is aborted, we need some covenant makers and covenant keepers. Saints step forward. In a culture in which individuals seek to acquire their own salvation, we need some messengers of God's redemption. Saints step forward.

The time has come for saints to step forward. That means you. Come out from your hiding places under the bushel baskets of institutions and in the saltcellars of culture. Remember the biblical call to sainthood is not a commission to hang upside down on some oriental cross but to live in Christ's name sitting at your typewriter, studying in a classroom, visiting in the dorm. The call to sainthood is not a summons to death in Christ's name in the coliseum in Rome but to life in Christ's name where you live. My challenge to you is not to attempt the spectacular, not to try the impossible, but to be faithful in the normal pursuits of life.

Both the church and the world are in need of contemporary saints. You—you are among the possibilities with whom God can work. Come out of your camouflage. Forsake your reticence. Just prior to this All Saints' Day, in the spirit of Martin Luther and for the glory of God, accept your identity, affirm your convictions, and take your stand. Saints, step forward!

A Reformation Spirit

John 2:13-16; Romans 3:21-26

"Here I stand; I cannot do otherwise. God help me. Amen." No doubt you recognize these memorable words from the Diet of Worms that have echoed across the ages. Hearing them brings to mind a bold little monk who stiffened his spine and for the sake of conscience stood against the entire hierarchy of the Roman Catholic Church. Admiration stirs and appreciation swells within us. A twinge of inspiration is entertained. "Oh, to be like that," we think. Each of us envisions those persons and institutions against which we would like to take our stands.

Be careful. Ripped from their historical context, Luther's words may sound like a statement of sheer defiance. You may conjure up images of an angered monastic on an unholy tear against all authority—a Vesuvian-like eruption of a long-latent hostility against the church. Such was not the case by any means.

Martin Luther's role in the reformation of the church cannot be understood properly apart from a recognition of his compassion for the church. By no stretch of the imagination did the monk from Wittenberg desire even to harm the church, much less to destroy it. His posting of the ninety-five theses was not a throwing down of the gauntlet to start a revolution but a lifting up of the truth to begin a conversation. Luther called for alterations only to affect purification and thus preservation. He endorsed much more than he condemned, affirmed far more than he negated.

Borrowing a beautiful analogy from Karl Barth, Roland Bainton likened Luther's experience to a man in the darkness climbing a winding staircase in the steeple of an ancient cathedral. In the blackness he reached out to steady himself and his hand laid hold of a rope. He was startled to hear the clanging of a bell.[1]

---

[1] Roland H. Bainton, *Here I Stand. A Life of Martin Luther* (New York: Abingdon Press, 1950) 83.

Reformation must be distinguished from rebellion and revolution, the work of termination and efforts at annihilation. In his cleansing of the Temple in Jerusalem, Jesus offered a complimentary model of reform. Driving out the money changers and overturning the merchants' stalls, the Lord sought not to destroy the Temple but to preserve it for its divine purpose as a house of prayer for all people.

The spirit of the Reformation was not a mean spirit of defiant destructiveness. Luther's spiritual kinfolks are not indignant iconoclasts bent on running roughshod over all that has been considered holy, lashing out at an institution which is despised, seeking to destroy every vestige of ecclesiastical authority. Rather, Luther's crowd is made up of children of the church motivated by a love for the church and a desire to strengthen its message, membership, and mission.

"Well, so what?" you ask. This is to be a sermon in a service of worship, not a lecture in some history course. What business do such observations have here even in proclamation related to a Reformation Sunday?

What happens institutionally also happens individually. Mistaken perceptions of the Reformation can result in serious mistakes in our personal situations. Truth is the concern of Christian proclamation.

Sooner or later, all of us conscientiously seek appropriate ways to relate to our pasts, to our traditions, to our families, to our churches. Particularly do we struggle with how to react to that which we consider wrong. We are tired of a faith encapsulated in clichés and protected from tough questions. We are weary of a simplistic, assembly-line evangelism obsessed with soul counts and oblivious to social concerns. We are fed up with petty moralisms that have more in common with cultural etiquette than with biblical ethics. We have had enough of glib, myopic answers to serious global questions. Aware that we are on our own as never before—forced to think for ourselves, free to make decisions individually—we see everything as up for grabs and seek to know what to do.

Precisely at this point I commend to you a reformation spirit—biblical in nature, verifiable in history. A bias toward destruction cannot be defended as an interest in reformation. In relation to our past, a reformation spirit arises from love, grows with appreciation, and labors toward strength not weakness. Faith is not abandoned, evangelism condemned, moral criteria rejected, and questions silenced. A secondhand faith is set aside in pursuit of a firsthand experience, a personal faith. Concern develops for a comprehensive evangelism that asserts that Christ is Lord *of all* or not Lord *at all*. Struggling with ethical dilemmas becomes more important than blindly accepting moral maxims. Serious responses are sought for abiding questions that must be answered.

A reformation spirit is crucial for us personally. To a great extent our lives are shaped by what we hold to and what we let go. In fact, the ebb and flow of our beings are built around our holding on to some things and letting go of others. To destroy everything indiscriminately is as harmful as to preserve everything uncritically. Knowing what to keep and what to turn loose is critical. A reformation spirit can help us.

Look at the following illustrations of that truth. A spirit of reformation involves

Investigation of Biblical Truths, Not Assertion of Self-Will

We best not forget the words that preceded Luther's infamous "Here I stand" declaration. The controversial priest's prior comment at Worms provided the explanation for all that followed—"My conscience is captive to the Word of God."[2] Martin Luther rejected the sales of indulgences and questioned certain exercises of papal authority not because of what he thought but because of what the New Testament taught. *Sola fide* was not an issue that Luther chose as the trumpet call for his personal work. Rather, the biblical truth of salvation by faith alone gripped Luther and catapulted him into action.

Shaped by a reformation spirit, we posture ourselves to listen to the Bible speak to us, not position ourselves to speak to the Bible or about the Bible. Most crucial in biblical interpretation is being addressed by a text, not addressing a text. What we say about the Bible is far less significant than what the Bible says about us.

A reformation spirit is needed amid much of the debate presently dividing major denominations. Though heralded as a true conservatism or a healthy fundamentalism, the contemporary movement has much in common with classic liberalism. Rationalistic statements of self-acclaimed human leaders are made more important than the faith-oriented declarations of the Bible. Contrary to a reformation spirit, efforts to recover the fundamental truths of scriptural texts are being supplanted by human-devised tests of orthodoxy centered on catchwords such as inerrancy and premillennialism.

---

[2]Ibid., 185.

Ironically, some of the major doctrinal insights of the reformation are now in trouble in the free-church tradition (of all places!). For example, belief in the priesthood of each believer—a means of affirming every person's accessibility to God—has been individualized with unjustifiable promises of human possibilities. Popularly expressed, a person claims, "I can read the Bible for myself and determine biblical truth. The Bible means what I think it means." That, my friends, is rank heresy! The Bible means what God says, not what we think.

True reformation involves renovation, not innovation. Luther's spirit is not one of self-assertion, pursuing my will, but one of biblical investigation, obedience to God's will. In vulnerable openness, perhaps with fear and trembling, we stand before the word of God in Scripture to discover truth for our convictions and the agenda for our lives.

Look on. A reformation spirit embraces

Appreciation for, Not Opposition to Tradition

True reformers seek to recapture what is best in their traditions. To understand a reformation spirit as an affront to tradition is to misunderstand. Every reformer lives in and from a tradition. Luther loved the tradition in which he worked.

Perceptive students of society now speak of a worldwide sense of historical dislocation which has developed because of a lack of connection with the vital and nourishing dimensions of tradition. Somewhere a destructive mentality equated coming of age with getting rid of tradition. Subsequently, we have suffered.

Tradition is bad only if it is a bad tradition. Again, crucial is an awareness of what to hold on to and what to let go of. A spirit of reformation spurs us to claim that which is best in our tradition. How we need again— personally and institutionally—the instruction of our heritage regarding the necessity of faith and reason, the importance of worship and work, the nurture of openness to new truth, and the preservation of convictions about belief-assertions.

Several years ago when the Tennessee Valley Authority was organized to provide low-cost electricity, stiff resistance developed in some remote sections of East Tennessee. Residents did not want the government to flood their "patches," the name given to their little farms. One citizen protested with great vehemence the government's intention to take his cabin "where the fire of my fathers has always burned." The practice was to bank the fires when not needed, and later to activate the coals so that "the fathers' fire" could be said never to have expired. Finally, a sensitive TVA staff member hit upon a plan which caused the patriarch to surrender. The living coals were placed in a huge oil drum and two men were assigned to keep fanning the fires as the coals were transported to a new house constructed for the family.[3]

What a good image of a true reformer. Tradition is appreciated, not opposed. A reformation spirit labors as well for the

Preservation, Not the Destruction of the Church

To be sure, Martin Luther never intended even a rift in the church, much less the emergence of new churches. True reform aims at preservation not destruction, renovation not innovation.

I am well aware of the temptations that hound us at this point. Apart from family pressures and accountability to longtime friends, we toy with the idea of giving up on the church. After all, from time to time we've been disappointed in it and disillusioned by it. Involvement has continued more out of routine than conviction.

Believe me, I do understand. I grow so impatient with sloppy preparation, insipid proclamation, and provincial missions. I tire of prophetic cowardice justified by the necessity of attention to a budget. I know that in many instances attending a meeting has been substituted for offering worship, talking about faith for exercising faith, and deliberating on ministry for doing missions.

Several years ago Canon Alexander of St. Paul's Cathedral in London announced that mathematical measurements indicated that St. Paul's Church was moving down Fleet Street at the rate of one inch every 100 years.[4] Immediately I thought that this also must be the pace of the larger church's progress morally, socially, and theologically. Needless to say, that movement hardly qualifies as deliberate speed.

---

[3]Brooks Hays, *Politics Is My Parish. An Autobiography* (Baton Rouge: Louisiana State University Press, 1981) 213.

[4]Richard A. Spencer, ed., *The Fire of Truth. Sermons by Raymond Bryan Brown* (Nashville: Broadman Press, 1982) 42.

I know the temptations. A reformation spirit is needed. We cannot dismiss the church or stand outside the church as true reformers. For all of my impatience with it and occasional anger toward it, I still love the church—universal and local. Despite its weaknesses, I do not want to get rid of it. Howard Thurman has expressed my sentiments, "There has not been a day since the beginning of the church that I have not been moved by its spirit."[5] Miraculously, the church teaches better than it acts, communicates strength even amid institutional weakness, and serves God regularly even as it stutters, fumbles, and trips along.

Reform is needed. But true reform is intended to recover the church, not to replace it or to displace it.

Of course, reform is an inadequate response in some situations. Some of you may have waited the entire sermon for that sentence. Sometimes a need exists for innovation, creation. But, please take care. I commend to you a reformation spirit that prevents us from throwing away what needs to be kept and from keeping what needs to be turned loose.

Learn from Luther who was instructed by the New Testament. Captivated by biblical truth, appreciative of but not bound by tradition, and committed to the church of Jesus Christ, we can assert our priorities for life and stake our claims in life. And, if a day of challenge comes to us, we will be ready to say in our own way, "Here, I stand, I cannot do otherwise. God help me. Amen."

---

[5]Howard Thurman, *With Head and Heart* (New York: Harcourt Brace Jovanovich, 1979) 162.